Table of Contents

KNOWLEDGE

- **Background**
- **Core Competencies**
- **Models of Recovery**
- **Ethics**

recovery[ri-kuhv-*uh*-ree]
noun, plural **re·cov·er·ies.**

- an act of <u>recovering</u>.
- the regaining of or possibility of regaining something lost ortaken away.
- restoration or return to health from sickness.
- restoration or return to any former and better state or condition.
- time required for <u>recovering</u>.

Background

History of Recovery

The concept of recovery can be traced back to the 1830's when John Perceval wrote of his personal recovery from psychosis in his book Perceval's Experience (Recovery within Reach, 2013). Despite the absence of formal peer recovery support resources in the 1870's, religious organizations such as the Women's Christian Temperance Union, the White, Red or Blue Ribbon Reform Clubs and the non-secular Keeley Institute and Keeley Leagues developed and embraced the peer recovery philosophy (Killeen, 2013). In the 1930's the recovery movement came into full swing in the substance abuse field with the development of Alcoholics Anonymous (AA), founded as a fellowship for people that were focused on sobriety from alcohol. This group was founded by Bill W. and is known as the largest peer recovery support group in the world. The mutual support group model goes back to the 1700's where groups of like-minded people would join together and make a pledge with each other to be sober. Even before this time, there was a "long and rich history of recovery within Native American tribes. In Recovery Circles, Native Americans shared their stories, joined together for the mutual support of the group, and elder members of the group reached out to aid newcomers." The model of an elder providing support for a newcomer has been around for hundreds of years and is the basic model that today's recovery coaching is founded upon. Recovery coaching is best described as an ongoing processional relationship between those seeking recovery and those that have successfully found the path to sobriety; often an intermediary between the client and treatment systems.

The process of recovery in the U.S., however, came to a standstill in the 1940's and 1950's when the primary model of treatment was institutionalization. Individuals were confined to state run hospitals, imprisoning them rather than rehabilitating them (Recovery within Reach, 2013). In the 1970's, the process of deinstitutionalization reduced the focus on hospitalization, and paved the way for a more community based approach. During the 1980's and 1990's, the Recovery Management model was brought to the forefront of addiction treatment and inspired change. In 2002, the President's New Freedom Commission on Mental Health led to a system wide shift in setting the goals of mental health and substance abuse services toward recovery in a way that makes treatment accessible and tailored to the needs of the people served.

What is Peer Support?

The concept of recovery coaching started out of William White's Recovery Management model and the 12 step/mutual support group model of recovery. Research supports the idea that recovery is facilitated by social support, which can be further broken down into emotional, informational, instrumental, and affiliational support (McLellan et al., 1998). Traditional mental health and substance abuse treatment facilities are limited in time, personnel and resources, leaving gaps in the aforementioned support services. Heavily influenced by funding, those providers concentrate on providing the services that will have the most impact in the shortest amount of time which often results in clients participating in groups and intensive therapy. These programs are also usually limited in the amount of time they can provide services, again, something dictated by those paying the bills. Successful recovery achieved in 28 days is unusual, so the dilemma for providers is how to structure treatment to ensure the best possible outcomes. Peer support and recovery coaches have become a cost effective way for providers to give clients a more comprehensive recovery experience as well as a connection to aftercare resources upon completion of formal treatment. SAMHSA (2009) further describes peer support as a "new kind of social support service designed to fill the needs of people in or seeking recovery." In addition to filling the gap during formal treatment it helps people stay engaged in the recovery process afterwards, decreasing the likelihood of a relapse. "Since they are designed and delivered by peers who have been successful in the recovery process, they embody a powerful message of hope, as well as a wealth of experiential knowledge. They can effectively extend the reach of treatment beyond the clinical setting into the everyday environment of those seeking to achieve or sustain recovery" (SAMSHA, 2009).

Research also suggests that those who manage their addiction as a chronic disease have success in a real recovery experience (Killeen, 2013) and we know support groups aid in chronic disease management. It may be this ability to extend services into the everyday life of the client that makes recovery coaching unique and successful.

Recovery coaches do not promote or endorse any particular way of achieving or maintaining sobriety, any particular 12-step program, or spiritual component of recovery. They focus on where the client "is at," allowing the client to create their vision of recovery in order to sustain recovery and live a meaningful life (Recovery Coaches International, 2013). The relationship between a client and recovery coach is dynamic and diverse. A coach may work with a client 24/7 for a month or have daily phone calls with the client. There is no set standard or "one size fits all" approach and the recovery coach has the ability to be flexible and use whatever methods will help the client in recovery.

There are also no prerequisites for becoming a recovery coach, except a passion to help those who are recovering from addiction (Killeen, 2013). Recovery coaches work in settings such as hospital emergency rooms, psychiatric hospitals, jails, prisons, homeless shelters, and nursing homes. They also work in community recovery centers, drop-in centers, clubhouses, the clients' home, and vocational placement agencies (Recovery to Practice, 2011).

Type of Support	Description	Peer Support Service Examples
Emotional	Demonstrate empathy, caring, or concern to bolster person's self-esteem and confidence.	Peer mentoring Peer-led supporting groups
Informational	Share knowledge and information and/or provide life or vocational skills training.	Parenting class Job readiness training Wellness seminar
Instrumental	Provide concrete assistance to help others accomplish task.	Child care Transportation Help accessing community health and social services
Affiliational	Facilitate contacts with other people to promote learning of social and recreational skill, create community, and acquire a scene of belonging.	Recovery centers Support league participation Alcohol- and drug-free socialization opportunities

Types of Peer Recovery Support and Service Examples

(SAMHA 2009)

Types of Recovery Coaches

Recovery coaches are as diverse as client needs dictate. This gives an aspiring coach flexibility to define their services, but the roles described below will provide an understanding of the types of recovery coaches that you will encounter.

Peer Recovery Support Specialist

The term peer recovery support specialist is often used interchangeably in the field with the terms recovery coach, peer mentor, recovery support practitioner, care manager or recovery support specialist. A peer recovery support specialist's primary goal is to help people achieve and maintain sustained recovery (Killeen, 2013). While there are both paid and unpaid positions, in most instances peer recovery support specialists volunteer their time. This, however, is expected to change with the Affordable Health Care Act, which may require hospitals, treatment centers and social service organizations to hire peer recovery support specialists, transforming it into a paid position.

The duties of a peer recovery support specialist vary. They will share their experiences of addiction and recovery, building an environment of trust and emotional support, helping the client develop goals and the terms of the client's recovery plan while providing social support to the client.

Travel or Sober Escort

Since transportation can be a significant challenge for a recovering addict, a travel escort or sober escort is a version of a recovery coach that may be required to transport a person in recovery (Killeen, 2013). Transportation may vary and it could be to bring the client to an appointment in town, take them to a court appointment or flying them across the country.

Long Term Recovery Coach or Sober Companion

The main difference between a recovery coach and the role of a long term recovery coach or sober companion is the time commitment. These individuals work full time with the client which might be for full 12 hour days, nights, weekends, or period of time where the coach is with the client for 24 hours of every day for an extended period of time (Killeen, 2013). This long term option might begin with a treatment discharge, supporting the client on their first day home, introducing the client to meetings, and guiding the client past triggers. This assignment might develop into a coaching relationship that continues further. With a long term recovery coach or sober companion nearby the client can be directed to make lifestyle changes that are supportive to a life in recovery.

Family Recovery Coach

"The family plays such an important role for a person in recovery, yet is so often neglected by traditional models of recovery" (Killeen, 2013). Beverly Buncher (2012),describesa family coach's role as helping "others deal with the challenges of living and working productively and happily, while 'being there' for an addicted loved one." A family recovery coaches' duties include helping the family to:

1. Experience inner peace and serenity whether the addict is still using or not
2. Help their loved one navigate the treatment world
3. Model centered living for the addict
4. Get their own life back
5. Accept their loved one, but not accept unacceptable behavior
6. Become an effective mirror for the addict
7. Function effectively at work and home, regardless of the addict's decisions

Telephone or Virtual Recovery Coach

This type of relationship can help a recovering client beyond face to face meetings. Many treatment centers are embracing virtual recovery coaching and these centers are providing a link to a recovery coach prior to discharge when the coach and client can connect face to face at the treatment center and then by telephone or internet after discharge. The type frequency and mode of contact depends on the client and recovery coach, but could be anything from a weekly web chat to a daily phone check in.

Intervention Coach

An intervention is a planned event in which those that care for an addict confront the addictand offer treatment. An intervention coach differs a bit from the other coaching roles since it is considered to be a health care profession and thus requires certification. A resource for those interested in certification is the National Association of Drugs and Alcohol Interventionist at http://www.nadai.us/ethics.php.

Legal Support Specialist

At times a lawyer may request a specific type of recovery coach to ensure that a client remains sober prior to or during a legal proceeding. These coachesare more likely to be licensed as Licensed Clinical Social Workers or Certified Alcohol and Drug Counselors (Killeen, 2013) as they usually require certifications to establish credibility as well as legal knowledge. Coaches with knowledge of the drug court system are particularly good for these positions. A legal support specialist may perform a client assessment defining the extent of the addiction, draft a letter to the court, offer treatment suggestions, and appear with the client in court.

A Coach to Detox a Home or Room

The role of this individual is as the name implies. It is a coach who is called in to search the room, home or apartment for substances. Additional training may be required to ensure proper collection and documentation procedures especially if it will be used in legal proceedings.

Core Competencies

Peer support and recovery coaching is still a new field and there is not a degree or standard training course available. There are guidelines put forth by reputable organizations to standardize the knowledge, skills and abilities required for successful coaching. Organizations that offer credentialing provide the public with an assurance that people credentialed have been trained according to the organization's standards and that members agree to abide by the ethical principles set forth by the organization. In addition to establishing professional credibility with future clients, professional organizations also give coaches networking and educational opportunities for professional growth. The International Coaching Federation (ICF) has set standards for coaching in general and offers a certificate program. Recovery Coaches International (RCI) focuses on recovery and provides members with education and resources specific to recovery coaching (RCI, 2013). They do not have a certificate program because they refer to ICF for coaching certificates, but they have put forth core competencies and a code of conduct that members are expected to uphold.

Othercore competencies for recovery coaches:

- Basic psychology
- Understanding of family and organizational systems
- Basic understanding of substance abuse, addiction and mental health
- History of coaching, current models and how coaching fits into current recovery models
- Understanding of current recovery models and the treatment systems in the area you wish to work
- Ethical principles of coaching and recovery coaching
- Phases and processes in coaching
- Self-awareness and knowledge of one's own recovery process
- Ability to create positive, supportive coaching relationships with proper boundaries
- Using communication skills, interviewing techniques and assessments to benefit the client
- Contracting, goal setting and recovery planning
- Advocacy, support, and the ability to connect clients to other services when needed

Most recovery coaches have gone through recovery themselves andknow what steps made recovery successful for them. In order to use that experience for the benefit of clients; however, they will need to blend their life skills with an understanding of the theory and practice of clinical addiction models and self-awareness (Killeen, 2013). The recovery coach must be able to guide a client through the recovery treatment process both emotionally and instrumentally. While the position of a recovery coach is non-clinical, familiarization with psychological language will help when working with therapists and other treatment providers.

Recovery coaches end up taking on many roles:

Outreach worker: Identifies and engages hard-to-reach individuals; offers living proof of the transformative power of recovery and what makes recovery attractive.

Motivator: Exhibits faith in client's capacity for change; encourages and celebrates their recovery achievements; mobilizes internal and external recovery.

Resources: Encourages the client's self-advocacy and economic self-sufficiency.

Ally and Confidant: The recovery coach genuinely cares and listens to the client; coaches can be trusted with confidences and can identify areas for potential growth.

Truth-Teller: Provides honest feedback on the client's recovery progress, identifying areas which have presented or may present roadblocks to continued abstinence.

Role Model and Mentor: The recovery coach offers their life as living proof of the transformative power of recovery and provides stage-appropriate recovery education.

Planner: Facilitates the transition from a professionally directed treatment plan to a client-developed and directed recovery plan, assisting in structuring daily activities around this plan.

Problem Solver: Helps resolve personal and environmental obstacles to recovery.

Resource Broker: Knowledgeable of resources for individuals and/or their families, is aware of sources of sober housing, can suggest employment that would be suitable for a person in recovery, can refer to health and social services, and offer additional recovery support that matches the client to particular support groups or 12-step meetings.

Monitor or Sober Companion: Sometimes a client will be best served with around the clock monitoring or companionship for a set number of hours per day, morphing the recovery coach's role into that of a sober companion. A sober companion can be available for travel in and out of the country

Tour Guide: Introduces newcomers into the local culture of recovery; provides an orientation to recovery; provides an orientation to recovery roles, rules, rituals, language, etiquette, and opens doors to the client for engagement in the recovery community. The recovery coach discusses a client's response to their therapeutic services or their mutual aid (12 steps) groups to enhance the client's engagement in recovery and reduce the possibility of attrition.

Advocate: Helps an individual and/or their families navigate the complex social service and legal systems.

Educator: A recovery coach provides a client with information about the stages of recovery, informing the client of professional helpers within the community, and instruct the client about the many pathways and life-styles of long-term recovery and after a relapse, the recovery coach provides recovery re-initiation education services.

In their position as a role model for successful recovery, the following values serve a coach well and become the basis for ethical decision-making in the recovery community (White, 2007)

Addiction Recovery Models

The Minnesota Model

The Minnesota Model was developed by Pioneer House, Hazelden, and Willmar State Hospital (White, 1998) and is heavily influenced by the 12-Step model, based on many of the same 12-Step principles. It is sometimes referred to as the 12-Step Model or the Disease Model. Below is an overview of the Minnesota Model:

1. Substance abuse is an involuntary, primary disease that is describable and diagnosable.

2. Substance abuse is a chronic and progressive disease, that without intervention, the signs and symptoms accelerate.

3. Substance abuse is not curable, but the disease may be arrested.

4. The nature of the substance user's initial motivation for treatment is not a predictor of outcome.

5. The treatment of substance abuse includes physical, psychological, social and spiritual dimensions.

6. The successful treatment of substance abuse requires an environment in which the user is treated with dignity and respect.

7. Alcoholics and addicts are vulnerable to abusing of a wide spectrum of mood altering drugs. This cluster of mood altering substances can be addressed through treatment that defines the problem as 'chemical dependency'.

8. Chemical dependency is best treated by a multi-disciplinary team whose members develop close, less formal relationships with their clients and whose activities are integrated within individualized treatment plans developed for each client. The recovery coach is a member of this team.

9. The focal point for implementing a treatment plan is assigning a primary counselor, usually a recovered person of the same sex and age group as the client, who promotes an atmosphere that enhances emotional self-disclosure, mutual identification and mutual support.

10. The most effective treatment for alcoholism includes orientation to a 12-Step mutual aid group like Alcoholics Anonymous (AA), with the expectation that the addict should work the 12-Steps, attend meetings that combine confrontation and support, attend recovery lectures, and employ one to one counseling to support the creation of a dynamic "learning environment".

11. The most viable ongoing sobriety-based support structure for clients following treatment is Alcoholics Anonymous.

12. Following these guidelines will enhance the recovery of people enmeshed in a variety of addictions including compulsive behavioral disorders.

When this model is used in practice common, interventions include group therapy, lectures, recovering persons as counselors, multi-disciplinary staff, therapeutic work assignments, family counseling, daily readings, presentation of a client's personal narrative, attendance at 12 step mutual aid groups and the opportunity for physical activity (Guthmann, 1999). These activities are highly structured and 12-Step mutual aid groups are viewed as an important component of aftercare.

A client participating in a recovery program based on the Minnesota Model focuses on chemical dependency as the primary problem and a first step in treatment is admitting that they are powerless over their addiction (Guthmann, 1999). Total abstinence from all substances is also required. This type of program provides the best possibilities for recovery when individuals physically dependent on substances will benefit from the support of a self-help group, and embrace a spiritual orientation.

Recovery Management Model (RM)

The Recovery Management Model (RM) is a newer model founded in 2006 by William White, and based on the concept that drug and alcohol addiction is a chronic and progressive disease similar to diabetes, allergies, high blood pressure and autoimmune diseases. Chronic diseases (including addiction) have the following features:

- Influenced by genetic heritability and other personal, family, and environmental risk factors
- Can be identified and diagnosed using well validated screening questionnaires and diagnostic checklists
- Are influenced by behaviors that begin as voluntary choices but evolve into deeply ingrained behaviors
- Patterns of behavior that, in the case of addiction, are further exacerbated by neurobiological changes in the brain that weaken volitional control over these contributing behaviors
- Are marked by patterns of onset that may be sudden or gradual
- Have a prolonged or permanent course that varies from person to person in intensity (mild to severe) and pattern (from constant to recurrent)
- Are accompanied by risks of profound pathophysiology (defined as an abnormal or undesired condition) disability, and premature death;
- Have effective treatments, self-management protocols, peer support frameworks, and similar remission rates, but no known definitive cure
- Often generate psychological responses that include hopelessness, low self-esteem, anxiety, and depression; and
- Generate excessive demands for adaptation by families and intimate social networks.

Treatingaddiction like a chronic disease, shifts treatment from the typical "admit, treat and discharge" mentality to a long term approach (Killeen, 2013). Using the RM model practitioners "would not view prior treatment as a predictor of poor prognosis or the grounds for denial of treatment admission. They would not convey the expectation that all clients should achieve absolute sobriety following a single, brief episode of treatment. They should not punitively discharge clients for becoming symptomatic, which means services would not be terminated due to a relapse."

The Harm Reduction (ATA) Model

One of the more controversial models of recovery is known as The Harm Reduction Model. It is sometimes difficult for health care providers to grasp because of the underlying philosophy that focuses on reducing the physical, social, and economic consequences despite continued substance use (Killeen, 2013). For example, the clean needle exchange programs and providing free condoms designed to decrease the spread of HIV are hallmarks of the Harm Reduction Model. Out of the Harm Reduction Model, Addiction Treatment Alternatives (ATA) was developed in 2000,specifically tailoring harm reduction to the substance abuse rehabilitation field.

The hallmark of this approach is that it aims to meet client's "where they are" in terms of their goals and personal needs (Killeen, 2013). While abstinence is a great goal, it is not viewed as the only goal in treatment with the ATA model. Practitioners working from the ATA framework believe in developing a strong relationship with the client. Focusing on strengths the client brings to the table engaging the client in a collaborative process of recovery.

- "Do No Harm" focuses not on the drug, but the harm done by the drug
- Exploration of the possible causes of the substance abuse in a person's background is important
- Using either the adaptive model, cognitive-behavioral or other models of recovery to meet the client "where they are"
- Focus on needs, affect, thought and behavior, not the substance addiction
- Any reduction in drug related harm is a success
- Work on techniques to reducing resistance and increasing motivation

12-step and other Mutual Aid Groups Model

The 12-step based approach is organized around the philosophy of Alcoholics Anonymous (AA). AA was founded by Bill W and Dr. Bob with the goal of developing a fellowship to stop drinking, but now consists of over 73,000 mutual aid groups' worldwide (Center for Substance Abuse Treatment, 1999). While AA does not view itself as a treatment modality, this approach has been the most prevalent model used in the U.S. over the last three decades and is often incorporated into other treatment methods. The foundation of this approach is to learn and practice the 12 Stepspublished in The Big Book(Alcoholics Anonymous, 2002):

1. We admitted we were powerless over alcohol that our lives had become unmanageable.

2. We came to believe that a Power greater than ourselves could restore us to sanity.

3. We made a decision to turn our will and our lives over to the care of God as we understood Him.

4. We made a searching and fearless moral inventory of ourselves.

5. We admitted to God, to ourselves, and to another human being the exact nature of our wrongs.

6. We were entirely ready to have God remove all these defects of character.

7. We humbly asked Him to remove our shortcomings.

8. We made a list of all persons we had harmed and became willing to make amends to them all.

9. We made direct amends to such people wherever possible, except when to do so would injure them or others.

10. We continued to take a personal inventory and when we were wrong promptly admitted it.

11. We sought through prayer and meditation to improve our conscious contact with God as we understood Him, praying only for knowledge of His will for us and the power to carry that out.

12. Having had a spiritual awakening as the result of these steps, we tried to carry this message to alcoholics and to practice these principles in all our affairs.

The application of these steps are personalized, incorporated into the client's daily life, and viewed as a model for change. A practitioner using this approach encourages their client to apply the 12-Step philosophies into daily living, share their experiences with others, ask for help when needed, and attend AA meetings on a regular basis. AA meetings are seen as a safe place away from the addiction and members are encouraged to find a group they can commit to attending.

AA relies heavily on sponsorship, another member with a foundation of sobriety providing newer members with guidance throughout the treatment process. In general, a sponsor is of the same gender as the client and will have more years of sobriety and recovery than the client. This allows them to have enough perspective on recovery and the implementation of the 12 steps.

The success of AA has spawned other mutual aid groups with different philosophies where members gather together and share their experiences. Leaders often donot have formal training, but rather speak from personal experience and members support each other within the common philosophical framework of the group. Mutual aid groups other than Alcoholics Anonymous include Narcotics Anonymous (NA), Overeaters Anonymous (OA) Gamblers Anonymous (GA), Al-Anon, Women for Sobriety, Save Our Selves, Life Ring Secular Recovery, Moderation Management and Alcoholics Victorious, SMART Recovery and faith based groups such as The Buddhist Recovery Network and Celebrate Recovery (Christian).

SAMHSA's Working Definition of Recovery

With the prevalence of co-occurring disorders and the variety of treatments available, the Substance Abuse and Mental Health Services Administration (SAMSHA) has served as a clearinghouse for research and treatment for patients and providers of behavioral health and recovery. In 2010, they gathered leaders in the fields of behavioral health and recovery to formulate a working definition of recovery and a set of unified principles for recovery. This effort, the Recovery Support Strategic Initiative, will serve to promote comprehensive treatment of mental health and substance use disorders.

Definition: A process of change through which individuals improve their health and wellness, live a self-directed life, and strive to reach their full potential.

Four Dimensions of Recovery:

- **Health**-abstinence from substances, managing other mental or physical ailments, nutrition, exercise
- **Home**-stable place to live
- **Purpose**-meaningful activities including education, employment, volunteerism, etc.
- **Community**-supportive relationships and social networks that promote healthy living

10 Guiding Principles of Recovery

- **Hope**-Belief that recovery is possible.
- **Person**-driven-Self-determination and self-efficacy are the foundation for success.
- **Many pathways**-Recovery is an individual, non-linear process.
- **Holistic**-Recovery needs to address the whole person as do services assisting with recovery.
- **Peer Support**-Social support through professionals, recovery coaches, mutual aid groups, families, churches, and communities are vital in supporting those in recovery.
- **Relational**-Increasing social resources and facilitating a sense of belonging promotes recovery.
- **Culture**-Values, traditions and beliefs are keys to sustaining the lifestyle change necessary for recovery
- **Addresses Trauma**-Healing unresolved trauma increases success in recovery.
- **Strengths/Responsibility**-Individuals have strengths to aid in their recovery and have a responsibility to cultivate them to support themselves and their communities in recovery.
- **Respect**-Many people have been affected by substance abuse and fostering an atmosphere of self-respect and respect for others in recovery requires great courage but also provides the kind of encouragement necessary for recovery.

Co-occurring disorders

According to the 2009 National Survey on Drug Use and Health (SAMSHA, 2009), 8.9 million adults with any mental illness also have a substance use disorder. Only 7.4 percent of them are receiving treatment for both conditions while 55.8 percent are not receiving any treatment at all. While more attention is being paid to providing appropriate treatment for co-occurring disorders, there are still far too many recovery and treatment centers that have not adopted services to meet the needs of both.

In addition to mental illness, a client's trauma history will also affect their recovery success. In 1998, SAMSHA commissioned the Women, Co-occurring Disorders and Violence Study, which was a comprehensive study on treatment utilization and effectiveness of women who presented for substance abuse treatment. They found that women who participated in this study presented for treatment an average of 14 times before their history of trauma was even factored into their recovery. These women had experienced interpersonal violence in some form since middle childhood and their substance use and mental health issues began in adolescence. When provided with trauma-informed interventions, the outcomes for recovery were much better and longer lasting. While this study focused on service delivery for women, it brought attention to the need for trauma-informed services and further changed the perspective of co-occurring disorders treatment. As a recovery coach, you may be the bridge between the client and finding the right recovery resources.

The assessments you do with a client will be important in connecting them with the right resources. Because of the high prevalence of mental illness and trauma, assume that your client will likely have one or both. How they answer your questions about the beginning of their substance use problems will indicate whether further comprehensive evaluation is necessary. For example, when assessing for stages of change, the client may express a desire to quit, but say that they are afraid to because the substance fulfills a need for them. Typical needs substances meet include helping with focus or calming down, numbing strong emotions, self-destruction, escape, increasing energy, or accomplishing tasks. They may also have a long history of recovery and relapse and low scores on the self-efficacy scale. You may ask them if they've experienced or witnessed events which scared them or caused them to fear for their life. If the answer is yes, it is highly likely that unresolved trauma will complicate recovery efforts.

An additional assessment that can be used is the Modified Mini Screen (Hazelden Foundation, 2013), which can either be self-administered or asked of a client in an interview format. This instrument screens for depression, suicidality, bipolar disorder, anxiety, social anxiety, obsessive and compulsive tendencies, PTSD, paranoia, hallucinations and delusions. If a client answers affirmatively to any of the questions, it is important to have them fully evaluated by a licensed mental health professional who specializes in co-occurring disorders. If your client has a history of trauma, it is especially important to have them evaluated and treated by someone with expertise in trauma-informed co-occurring disorder treatment.

Licensed mental health providers who specialize in trauma-informed co-occurring disorder treatment are trained to treat the mental illness, trauma and substance abuse at the same time. The treatment and recovery plan should be all inclusive, meaning the client's work with the recovery coach will complement their work with a counselor and, if appropriate, the psychiatrist prescribing medications.

According to Dual Recovery Anonymous (2009), a 12-step mutual aid group for people with co-occurring disorders, states a variety of problems are possible as a result of a co-occurring disorder.

- Psychiatric symptoms may be covered up or masked by alcohol or drug use.
- Alcohol or drug use or the withdrawal from alcohol or other drugs can mimic or give the appearance of some psychiatric illness.
- Untreated chemical dependency can contribute to a reoccurrence of psychiatric symptoms.
- Untreated psychiatric illness can contribute to an alcohol or drug relapse.

Other problems and consequences that are associated with co-occurring disorders include:

- Family problems or problems in intimate relationships.
- Isolation and social withdrawal.
- Financial problems.
- Employment or school problems.
- High risk behavior while driving.
- Multiple admission for chemical dependency services due to relapse.
- Multiple admissions for psychiatric care.

- Increased emergency room admissions.
- Increased need for health care services.
- Legal problems and possible incarceration.
- Homelessness

It is tempting to figure out which came first, the substance use disorder or the mental health problems. There are many different philosophies and it's important for a recovery coach to understand how a counselor will approach co-occurring recovery with your client. As mentioned previously, the relationships a client has with the recovery support team is essential to success and that includes how you work with mental health professionals to whom you refer your clients.Individuals living with mental illness may be more sensitive to the effects of alcohol and other drugs (National Alliance on Mental Illness, 2013), and those substances can exacerbate the symptoms of their mental health disorder. In some cases the person may have turned to substances as a way to control and self-medicate their mental health symptoms. Regardless of the order, the use of substances with a mental health disorder can create a perpetuating negative feedback loop which is difficult to disrupt. The focus should be present-focused on treatment and recovery and as a recovery coach, you will have more opportunities to observe and recognize behaviors in your client that can be brought to the attention of their mental health provider

Medication Assisted Treatment (MAT)

There are several opportunities and challenges for clients in recovery and the use of medication is attractive for managing mental health issues as well as substance use issues. There are many providers who will prescribe medication for mental health disorders, but fewer are qualified to prescribe for co-occurring disorders. The American Society of Addiction Medicine (2013) is a professional society that offers training and credentials to physicians specializing in addiction medicine, and their mission is to promote comprehensive recovery for clients with the understanding of the roles counselors and recovery coaches play. ASAM credentialed physicians understand the nature of addiction as a chronic disease, the interactivity of psychotropic medication and substance specific medication, and the psychological factors related to using medication in recovery.

Medications for alcohol dependence (SAMHSA, 2013)

Naltrexone (ReVia®, Vivitrol®, Depade®): In pill form or monthly injectable, Naltrexone blocks the "high" of drinking thereby diminishing cravings and assists in resisting the urge to drink. Provider must be licensed to prescribe.

Disulfiram (Antabuse®): Interferes with the body's ability to metabolize alcohol, causing unpleasant side effects when alcohol is ingested. Client must take pill daily in order for it to work and compliance can be an issue.

Acamprosate Calcium (Campral®): Assists with physical and emotional discomfort of withdrawal.

Medications for opioid dependence

Methadone: Blocks the effects of opiates and when tapered, can ease withdrawal symptoms and cravings. Administered by licensed providers and length of treatment is at least one year.

Buprenorphine (Suboxone® and Subutex®): In pill form or sublingual tablet, it blocks the effects of opiates and eases withdrawal symptoms. Progression through all three treatment phases can take a year or more and there are more risks for interactions with psychotropic drugs as well as addiction to buprenorphine itself. Providers are licensed, regulated, and limited in the number of of clients per provider.

Naltrexone: pill form or monthly injectable blocks the "high" of using opiates which diminishes craving and assists in resisting the urge to use. Provider must be licensed to prescribe.

Benefits of MAT

- Improve survival
- Increase retention in treatment
- Decrease illicit opiate use
- Decrease hepatitis and HIV seroconversion
- Decrease criminal activities
- Increase employment
- Improve birth outcomes with perinatal addicts

Barriers and challenges of using MAT

- Accessibility: ASAM qualified medical providers trained to treat clients with co-occurring disorders are difficult to find.
- Availability: Prescribers are monitored and regulated by government agencies who limit the number of clients per provider which limits availability of medications such as buprenorphine and naltrexone.
- Cost: Psychotropic medications and addiction specific medications are expensive, and most will require long-term use to ensure positive outcomes. Not all insurances will cover substance related medications and those that do have strict guidelines that must be followed by the client and the provider. If medications are covered, there may also be limitations in the length of time a client can use them which may be in conflict with actual time needed for recovery.
- Compliance: There is stigma attached to using medication and clients may have to deal with the implication of substituting one drug for another. Some treatment models and recovery communities who are abstinence based may not welcome clients utilizing MAT. Clients may also have difficulty adjusting behaviorally to new daily habits that may be in conflict with addiction habits.
- Comprehensiveness: The importance of a comprehensive treatment team for clients in MAT cannot be stressed enough. The treatment/recovery plan should be shared between all providers and all providers should be in regular communication with each other and with the client. None of these interventions work alone, rather, they complement each other.

Recovery coaches can be integral in connecting a client to quality providers. Look for providers who have the best credentials and who will work within a treatment team that has the client's goals for recovery in mind. Establish relationships in advance so you can educate your clients and be an advocate for the client. When guiding clients through MAT, the added dimensions of accessing the right providers, navigating the policies involved with paying for and securing the medication, as well as keeping the client from becoming complacent or fully reliant upon medication can affect recovery in positive and negative ways. A good recovery coach can help relieve some of that stress.

Ethics

The ethical delivery of services is important not only to the success of the client, but also the coach. The professional organizations in the peer support and coaching field provide guidelines for professional relationships, confidentiality and ethical decision-making, all in the interest of "doing no harm" to clients and the profession.

Professional conduct in relationships includes communicating honestly and clearly with a client, setting expectations and limitations in advance, treating everyone involved with a client's recovery with dignity and respect, and maintainingprofessional boundaries. As a helper, it's tempting to do everything possible to help a client and it's tempting to get "sucked in." Establishing boundaries early with clients protects both parties and sets up a model of a healthy professional relationship from which the client can learn and apply to other relationships.

Boundaries

An example of a boundary may include limiting communication to certain hours of the day, consistent with the terms of the contract. If a coach is providing support with weekly face-to-face meetings, it is important to explainappropriate communication in advance. Giving a client permission to contact 24/7 may not be in the best interest of the coach or the client. The coach needs personal time and the client needs to learn how to work through issues that come up and not rely on the coach as a "rescuer."

Interpersonal boundaries are another important ethical consideration. Before a coach assesses the client in the first session, the client will assess the coach. Recovery coaches who are in recovery themselves have an added responsibility to ensure that the coaching relationship is about the client's recovery, not their own. While friendship with a client is important, be careful to maintain proper boundaries in the release of personal information. It may be helpful for a client to know that you are in recovery, but keep the information shared to that which will help the client with their recovery. Clients are perceptive and will be able to detect if the relationship will be more about the coach than the client. The best way to prevent or catch softening of boundaries is for the coach to have a mentor, supervisor or other professional to help keep the coach accountable.

Another example of professional conduct is setting clear terms and expectations up front and remaining consistent throughout the coaching relationship. The professional organizations stress the important of written agreements. If something is not in writing, it is difficult to uphold or enforce it. For example, including things in your contract that explain the coach's role and the limits of that role, what the client's responsibilities are, what financial obligations are expected and how they will be handled, how success will be measured, and how the coaching relationship can or will be terminated. If there are any changes during the course of the coaching relationship, those changes must also be agreed upon in writing. For example, if a client requires transportation assistance 2 months after the coaching relationship begins, a coach may offer to provide transportation until the client is able to provide their own. A written transportation agreement may include how often a coach is willing and able to transport, where a coach is willing to go, who is paying for expenses related to transport, how long transport will be offered, as well as client goals for transportation independence.

Professional limitations

Peer support and recovery coaches are in a unique position to do a lot of good in clients' lives. However, providing help within the context of your training and expertise dictates that coaches have enough self-awareness to know their own limits and when it's appropriate to refer a client for other services.

For example:

Recovery coach (RC) is NOT a:	You are moving beyond the boundaries of the recovery coach role if you:
Sponsor (or equivalent)	• Perform AA/NA or other mutual aid group service work in your RC role • Guide someone through the steps or principles of a particular recovery program
Therapist/Counselor	• Diagnose • Provide counseling or refer to your support activities and "counseling" or "therapy" • Focus on problems/"issues"/trauma as opposed to recovery solutions
Nurse/Physician	• Suggest or express disagreement with medical diagnoses • Offer medical advice • Make statements about prescribed drugs beyond the boundaries of your training and experience
Priest/Clergy	• Promote a particular religion/church • Interpret religious doctrine • Offer absolution/forgiveness • Provide pastoral counseling

(White, 2007)

Clients and other treatment providers will appreciate a coach's acknowledgement of limitations. Establish relationships with other providers with whom you can work symbiotically and have those referral sources ready.

Another professional limitation to be aware of is that of dual relationships with clients. A professional relationship is one between a client and coach for the purpose of recovery. It is prohibited for licensed professionals in helping fieldsto have personal, sexual and business relationships clients. The rules for peer recovery support specialists and recovery coaches are less strict; most stating they are discouraged if they interfere with the ability to provide good services to the client. However, consistency within the helping fields make it easier for clients and for the emotional and professional safety of the coach, these boundaries are strongly encouraged.

Confidentiality and Privacy

For providers of substance abuse services, there are multiple layers of confidentiality of which to be aware. The exact rules and policies will depend upon the system and state a recovery coach or peer specialist is working within; however, it is wise and in accordance with ethics put forth by professional organizations for entrepreneurial coaches to follow the same rules.to keep things simple for clients and to cover the coach.

Ethical confidentiality

Confidentiality rules are outlined in ethics standards and codes of conduct for professional associations as well as written into state regulations. In general, these rules and standards state that what happens within the coaching or peer support relationship stays within that relationship and can only be released with written permission from the client. There are also rules for which confidentiality can be broken without client consent, such as if a client becomes a danger to self or others, if child abuse is reported, in an emergency situations, or with court orders. Each state has different requirements and these limits to confidentiality should be outlined in the coaching agreement and discussed at the very beginning of the coaching relationship.

When working with minors, families, or other supporters of the client, it is especially important to put your policies in writing and express them clearly. It is generally accepted by professionals working in recovery to maintain the confidentiality of the client in all situations. In other words, communicating with family members without the client's knowledge is frowned upon and has a good chance of damaging your coaching relationship with the client. For example, if something needs to be communicated to family members or supporters, it is recommended to encourage the client to communicate that information. The coach can be there for support or to facilitate communication.Not only are you maintaining your professionalism with the client, but as a facilitator, it can help the client feel empowered as they navigate through difficult communications.

Often, peer recovery support specialists are asked to facilitate support groups. Groups are effective for practicing relationshipand communication skills, for building a support community, and normalizing the challenges encountered in recovery. Confidentiality is especially difficult in groups and should be addressed early in the group process. In groups, the clients hold confidentiality. The peer recovery support specialist is bound by confidentiality rules and laws, but clients are not. It is recommended that clients be made aware of this. Often, a condition of group attendance is that clients agree to respect the confidentiality of other members. This confidentiality extends to outside of the meeting location including social media sites. For example, clients should be advised not to post anything about group meetings or group meeting topics on Facebook.Interactions in public places should remain anonymous as well unless otherwise agreed upon by group members. For example, if members see each other in the grocery store, are they comfortable saying hello? Some people in recovery are not comfortable with others knowing, therefore, if another group members says "hello" in public, it may be awkward for the other member to explain how the members know each other.

HIPAA

While the previous section discussed ethical principles and rules, HIPAA is a privacy law that is enforceable and punishable with fines and prison time (Freedman &McCaughan, 2008). The law itself is rather complicated, but it is generally accepted in the helping professions to err on the side of caution and maintain compliance even if a business or helping entity may not be required to adhere to the rules and regulations. Not only does it cover an entity in terms of compliance, but it also legitimizes the entity and promotes professionalism and client confidence.

There is a section of HIPAA that pertains to communicating with third party payers and another that handles administrative security. This guide will focus on the two rules that are most relevant to coaches, The Privacy Rule and The Security Rule.

The Privacy Rule covers anything that can identify an individual, referred to as PHI (personal health information). First, you are not to release any PHI without the consent of your client, and second, you must keep a record of all disclosures. You must also have privacy policies and procedures in written form and available to clients upon request.

The Security Rule covers administrative, physical, and technical privacy. The HIPAA law is very specific about these safeguards and includes policies and procedures that clearly show how you comply with the HIPAA law. Regular training should be included in the plan as should contingency plans, internal audits, and how you will handle security breaches. If you work with outside vendors that could have access to PHI, they must also be HIPAA compliant and have signed agreements to that effect. Finally, the physical safeguards used must be outlined as well. Physical safeguards include how hardware and software will be introduced, maintained and removed in a secure fashion. Methods include the double-lock rule, meaning employees have to get through 2 locks or 2 layers of security to get to PHI; keeping PHI away from any eyes not authorized to view it which includes computer screens, files, check-in lists, etc. Technical safeguards must also be in place to protect digital data including phone lines, computer systems, mobile phones, faxes, and emails.

The bad news is compliance is taken seriously and violations are strict. The good news is that the Office of Civil Rights has a lot of the materials you need on their website, including sample agreements, policies, procedures and audit plans.

42 CFRPart 2

In addition to HIPAA, those providing substance abuse recovery services also have to comply with Federal Rule 42 CFR Part 2. Basically, this regulation states that no information about a client's identity, diagnosis, prognosis or treatment can be disclosed without written permission. Some exceptions are allowed under the law to comply with state and federal law, but it is generally acceptable to not even identify that a client is a client under this regulation (Kunkel, 2012).

Confidentiality and privacy laws can be complicated, but a good rule is to maintain the highest level of confidentiality possible. This includes keeping paper and electronic records secure, being aware of where meetings are held and who will be thereand getting the client's written permission for anything that could be construed as a violation of any of the above including consultations with supervisors or other providers.

Documentation

Good documentation is essential: "if it isn't documented, it didn't happen." Documentation is important not only to protect you as a recovery coach, but it is required by insurance companies and Medicare to monitor the client's progress and justify expenses. In addition, other professionals on the treatment team may rely on your notes. Clients involved with other mental health services, physicians, probation/parole officers, drug court, Child Protection Services, or the Intoxicated Driver programs may rely on your notes to show program compliance, progress, etc.

What you put into a note is just as important as what you leave out. Keep in mind who will be reading the notes and will likely follow the client in their permanent health or legal record. Keep notes fact based, related to the client's stated goals, and progress toward those goals. For example, if a client is making progress toward a goal on boundaries and cutting ties with previous substance-involved relationships, there is no need to detail an argument that resulted in a physical altercation. It is sufficient to note that client successfully cut ties with a substance-using relationship.

A simple note format to use is called D.A.P. The letters of D.A.P. are an easy way to remember what needs to be included in a well-developed progress note. D stands for data, A for assessment and P for plan. Below is an outline to follow when using the D.A.P. method.

Data- Subjective and objective data about the client

- Subjective - what client can said or said they felt (always use direct quotes)
- Objective – observable behavior
- Content discussed and progress towards goals
- Was homework completed and reviewed?

Assessment – What is going on?

- Working hypotheses on client status in recovery
- Results of any tests, screening tools or assessments
- Response to treatment (example "more involved…")

Plan - Response or revision

- What you are going to do next, based on client's response to treatment
- Goals and objectives addressed / accomplished during this session
- Next session date
- Any topics to be covered in next session(s), and homework given

The following checklist can be used to ensure that you are developing well written documents.

- Think about what you are going to write and formulate before you begin
- Be sure you have the right file!
- Date and sign every entry
- Proofread
- Record as "late entry" anytime it doesn't fall in chronological order; be timely
- Think about how the client comes through on paper
- Watch abbreviations-use only those approved
- Errors should have a line through incorrect information. Write error, initial and date
- Write neatly and legibly; print if handwriting is difficult to read
- Use proper spelling, grammar and sentence structure
- Don't leave blank spaces between entries; can imply vital information left out
- Put client name/case number on each page
- Avoid slang and curse words
- Write so another provider can continue quality care from these notes
- Use descriptive terms
- Describe what you observed, not your opinion of what you observed
- Use power quotes: For example: "Client remains at risk for _____ as evidenced by _____" "The current symptoms include _____" "The client has shown limited progress in _____"

CREATING PARTNERSHIP

Background

- **First meeting**
- **Assessments**

Creating Partnership

A coaching or peer recovery support relationship is unique in that it is closer and more intensive than a therapeutic relationship, but professional detachment is still required. Research by Castonguay, Constantino and Holtforth (2006), showed how significant the relationship is for clients in counseling, which can be generalized to all those in helping roles. More importantly, however, is that it is the client's perception of the relationship that is the best predictor of outcome for recovery success.

What does a successful therapeutic relationship look like?

- The client feels like a priority. Meetings are about them, conversation is about them, plans are about them. The helper listens, validates, and normalizes.
- The client is able to trust the person helping. The helper is a living example of being honest, up front about expectations, firm with boundaries, and doing what they say they are going to do and holds the client to the same behaviors.
- The client is valued for who they are. The helper distinguishes the character and personality of the client from behavior the client engaged in while using.
- The client begins to see themselves positively through the helper. The helper is an encourager, a cheerleader, pointing out strengths and positive progress.
- Recovery is client-driven. The helper does not lead the client, the helper is on the journey side by side with the client with the client feeling empowered to call the shots. The helper should not work harder than the client.

There are several skills a recovery coach can use to solidify a trusting relationship with a client. The primary skill is active listening. Armstrong (2006), explains that active listening is more than just what is being said, but it is also how it is being said that is important. It allows the client to note you are interested, keeps them focused on the topic and encourages them to talk more (Egan, 2010). It also strengthens the professional relationship while building rapport. A client will know when you are actively listening by your posture, body position, head nods, facial expressions, gestures, and verbal encouragement. A recovery coach should focus attention on the client, be nonjudgmental, resist distractions, and reflect back to the client what is heard in order to validate the client's feelings and desires (Kottler& Brown, 2000).

The value of peer support and recovery coaching goes beyond guiding a client through recovery and supporting them through obstacles. The power of peer support is in the living example of successful recovery through everyday living. When a coach keeps commitments, interacts with others nonjudgmentally, maintains healthy boundaries with others, advocates for a client, encourages a client, and continues to stay away from substances themselves the client begins to see the possibility of living that way themselves.

First meeting

Initial contact with the client can cause stress or anxietyfor both the client and the recovery coach. Many times clients do not know what to expect. You will want to be sure to set the proper tone for them even before the first meeting. It is suggested that the recovery coach provide the client with a definition of coaching and the time frame for which coaching will take place (Killeen, 2013). This information can be distributed through a brochure, information on the coach's website, or written directly into a coaching contract. Before the initial meeting, a recovery coach may also request information from the client in the form of a questionnaire. This questionnaire can help determine what the client expects to receive from the coaching relationship and should be completed prior to the initial session.

The first meeting is a critical step in the process. At this stage there is a logical development that a recovery coach and a client must go through in order to solve any problem (Egan, 2010). The first stage, is called the "current picture" in which the recovery coach learns about the client's current situation, key issues, motivation for change, and resources needed. It is also at this point that a trusting relationship is developed which will be the foundation of the recovery coach/client relationship (Egan, 2010).

One way to get a current picture is to have the client create a personal narrative. Mitchell (2002),writes that "we are our stories, our accounts of what happened to us," thus "no stories, no self." This concept is the epitome of personal narrative therapy which is a form of psychotherapy based upon the belief that we all have a unique story to tell. With personal narrative therapy clients are highly encouraged to narrate their personal life story which is often referred to as their 'autobiographical self' (Pawelczyk, 2011). Through the use of storytelling techniques, this exercise is away to give meaning to the past. Using this approach, a coach can see how a client's life is highly influenced by their family, culture and social circles. (Center for Substance Abuse Treatment, 1999).

This technique was originally developed by Michael White and his colleague David Epston for clients in therapy to recall events of their life and it has an important application in recovery as well (Killeen, 2013). In regard to the recovery field, personal narratives play dual purpose in the journey towards recovery and are a way that clients can see how they organized their lives around specific events. It allows clients to 1) take ownership of past behavior and 2) to develop self-insight. Both are important general goals for those in recovery. This technique also has a dual purpose of allowing a recovery coach to gain deep insight into the client as a whole. By learning what a client is willing to reveal about their life events, the recovery coach is able to truly learn their story.

This technique is often used in treatment centers and in traditional talk therapy. By allowing client's to author their life story, their life becomes meaningful and allows the client to take ownership by breaking old patterns and developing new solutions (Center for Substance Abuse Treatment, 1999). It is by no means an easy task. Often this is the first time that clients have sat down and documented their early childhood experiences and it may bring up a storm of emotions. Killeen (2013) suggests that if the narrative takes more than two weeks to write,a client is showing resistance which should be noted and discussed further.

To further apply the narrative approach in the recovery field you might ask your client, "How has substance abuse influenced your life?" or "Have there been times when you did not allow addiction to take over?" Such questions can help recognize positive aspects and potential resources that can be enhanced, as well as deficits that must be conquered (Center for Substance Abuse Treatment, 1999).

According to Brief Interventions and *Brief Therapies for Substance Abuse* by the Center for Substance Abuse Treatment, narrative therapy helps clients resolve their problems by:

- Helping them become aware of how events in their lives have assumed significance
- Allowing them to distance themselves from impoverishing stories by giving new meaning to their past
- Helping them to see the problem of substance abuse as a separate, influential entity rather than an inseparable part of who they are (note there is a discrepancy between this theory and the use of the introductions by AA member's; "My name is Jane, and I am an alcoholic")
- Collaboratively identifying exceptions to self-defeating patterns
- Encouraging them to challenge destructive cultural influences they have internalized
- Challenging clients to rewrite their own lives using an alternative and/or a preferred script

If a client is able to write the personal narrative prior to the first meeting, it will give the coach a better idea of how to proceed with further assessments. If it is a difficult process for the client, it may be better for them to write the personal narrative after securing coaching and counseling support. It's important to remember that many people who struggle with substance abuse have trauma histories which can trigger strong feelings and lead to relapse. Trust your instincts with clients. If they are hesitant to do a personal narrative, there may be a good reason and may be a sign to connect them with a counselor.

Assessment

Assessment basics

Assessment is a broad term used in social sciences to describe an "ongoing and cyclical process of observation, inference, and hypothesis testing with the goal of building an accurate, but tentative and fluid client model (Spengler et al, 1995)." This process involves interviewing clients, talking with other providers, observing client behavior, and administering tests. All of these things are important to create a picture of your client but they are meant to be used together; no one piece of information can be the sole source of information.

You may be the first point of contact with a client, you may come into contact with a client while they are in treatment, or shortly after. If you are the first point of contact, the thoroughness with which you assess a client and share information with other providers will not only benefit the client by getting them what they need quicker, but it will also be helpful in establishing your credibility as a recovery coach. If you are in contact with a client further into the treatment process, check with providers for assessments and request access to the information. Then, you can make decisions whether to duplicate any instruments and what other instruments could be helpful to the client.

Assessments are also used in the treatment community to determine levels of care and justify the continued expense of treating a client. For example, providers who are paid by insurance or other third party payers, will classify clients as inpatient, intensive outpatient, outpatient, or aftercare. Definitions of these levels of care differ and are influenced by state law and payer policies. Payment for each level of care is often authorized for a length of time determined by the payer and justification is needed for treatment continuation or transition to the next level. Each treatment provider will have its own protocol, but there are generally "level of care placement criteria" which are determined through the use of standardized assessment instruments. By using similar assessment models in recovery coaching, you will be able to facilitate relationships with other providers and provide a continuity of care to clients. There may also be a time when recovery coaching will be included in third party payer systems, which will require you to justify the need for your services.

Before diving into assessment; however, it's important to have a good foundation. Understanding why and how you are going to evaluate clients will not only help you provide quality services to your client, but it will also help the client understand themselves in an empowering way.

Purposes of assessment

- To gather information, learn about client, establish a relationship
- To determine goals and objectives that can be measured
- To measure client functioning against norms
- To determine symptoms and/or symptom severity to support further treatment recommendations
- To measure client progress throughout recovery

Assessment ethics

- ***Know yourself.*** You will be teaching clients about self-awareness and it is imperative that you lead by example. Knowledge of your own biases will protect you from boundary violations and will prevent you from extending yourself outside of your level of experience.

- ***Know the instruments you are using and be prepared to explain them.*** Take the assessments yourself, look into the research that supports their findings, and understand why they are important to the recovery process. Learn them well enough so you can explain them to clients in plain language.

- *Are the instruments you want to use valid* (measure what they say they measure) and reliable (can the instrument be repeated with the same results)? The checklists in magazines are not credible instruments of assessment. To be taken seriously by professionals in the recovery field, use instruments that can be used in other aspects of the client's treatment.

- *What qualifications and training are necessary to administer the instrument?* There are differences between instruments that require specialized training and instruments available free online. Both are beneficial as long as it is clear to the client that the results are suggestions. What will be important to the client is the level of discovery, knowledge, and empowerment gained from taking the instruments. For example, the Myers-Briggs Type Inventory (MBTI) is a terrific instrument for enhancing a client's understanding of themselves, but to get excellent results, it is best administered and interpreted by a qualified professional. This costs money, which clients may not be interested in spending. There is, however, a free version available online called the Jung Typology Test, which is the foundational theory for the MBTI. Is it exact? No, but it will get the client started in self-exploration.

- *Present results to clients in a nonbiased, multicultural context.* The way results are interpreted will influence how a client receives the information. Clients may interpret results as "bad" or "negative" but you have an opportunity to reframe them in a more positive, nonbiased, nonjudgmental way. It's also important to understand that not all assessments are culturally appropriate. Some personality instruments may convey judgment, favoring characteristics or traits which may not make sense for your clients. Good assessment instruments will be nonbiased and they will take culture into account.

- *Are you duplicating assessments already done? Will they complement other providers?* If you are part of a client's treatment team, talk to the other providers about assessments that have been done and what your ideas are for assessing a client. You may choose to repeat an assessment to determine progress, to clarify, or to verify previous information, but nothing is more exasperating to a client than repeating assessments when meeting another provider.

- *How will the assessment be used?* Be able to explain to a client the purpose for using the information gathered from the assessment process. Some are good for exploration, some are good for building recovery capital and measuring progress, while others are good for screening for other problems. The client needs to know that all this collected information will be used for their benefit.

- *Documentation* of assessments is important. As stated in the documentation module, if it isn't documented, it didn't happen.

Characteristics of good assessors

- Patient
- Good communication
- Awareness of bias
- Good listening skills
- Skeptical
- Pays attention to nonverbal data
- Curious
- Open-minded
- Persistent
- Develops rapport
- Delays judgment

Motivational Interviewing

According to Miller and Rollnick (1991), the overall goal of the first session is to identify the client's stage of change. Motivational Interviewing (MI) focuses on exploring a client's intrinsic motivations for change and resolving ambivalence in a way that is congruent with the client's values and concerns. It's more of a collaborative conversation about change designed to strengthen a client's motivation and commitment to change. MI research suggests that those clients who create their own meaning for change are more likely to succeed in lasting change.

Principles and techniques of MI

- Collaboration (not confrontation)
  - Expressing empathy
- Evocation (drawing out, rather than imposing ideas)
  - Rolling with resistance and developing discrepancy
- Autonomy (not authority)
  - Supporting self-efficacy

MI is less of an assessment technique than it is a style of talking with a client throughout a coaching relationship. During the assessment phases, the helper listens for "change talk" to determine a client's stage of change and then guides the client through change talk. When a client talks about change, they may say things like "I want to change," "I should change, but I don't know what to do," "If I don't change, bad things will continue to happen." A helper would then use techniques such as asking open ended questions, exploring goals and values, asking for elaboration or coming alongside a client. The more a client talks about change in a positive way, the more likely positive change will occur.

Cognitive Distortions

There are numerous challenges encountered in every stage of working with a recovering client. A well prepared recovery coach can anticipate reluctance in discussing the topic of addiction or exploring the reasons for certain feelings with their client. Common psychological defenses such as denial, minimizing, sidetracking, and avoidance will appear in their discussions. An example of sidetracking during a conversation with the client is when the topic changes immediately to the client's child and their problem with a math homework assignment as the client is sharing some deep intimate feelings about their history. An example of minimizing is when the client has been arrested for shoplifting and the client defends themselves by saying it should be dismissed because her offense was stealing a hat that only cost $15 (Killeen, 2013).

15 Common Cognitive Distortions by John Grohol (2009), lists and defines common distortions. Below are the top 10 taken in whole from this source.

1. Filtering.

We take the negative details and magnify them, while filtering out all positive aspects of a situation. For instance, a person may pick out a single, unpleasant detail and dwell on it exclusively, so that their vision of reality becomes darkened or distorted.

2. Polarized Thinking (or "Black and White" Thinking).

In polarized thinking, things are either black-or-white, and never gray. We have to be perfect or we're a failure — there is no middle ground. You place people or situations in "either/or" categories, with no shades of gray or allowing for the complexity of life. If your performance falls short of perfect, you see yourself as a total failure.

3. Overgeneralization.

In this cognitive distortion, we come to a general conclusion based on a single incident or a single piece of evidence. If something bad happens only once, we expect it to happen over and over again. A person may see a single, unpleasant event as part of a never-ending pattern of defeat.

4. Jumping to Conclusions.

Without individuals saying so, we know what they are feeling and why they act the way they do. In particular, we are able to determine how people are feeling toward us. For example, a person may conclude that someone is reacting negatively toward them but doesn't actually bother to find out if they are correct. Another example is a person may anticipate that things will turn out badly, and will be convinced that their prediction is already an established fact.

5. Catastrophizing.

We expect disaster to strike, no matter what. This is also referred to as "magnifying or minimizing." We hear about a problem and use what if questions (e.g., "What if tragedy strikes?" "What if it happens to me?"). For example, a person might exaggerate the importance of insignificant events (such as their mistake, or someone else's achievement). Or they may inappropriately shrink the magnitude of significant events until they appear tiny (for example, a person's own desirable qualities or someone else's imperfections).

6. Personalization.

Personalization is a distortion where a person believes that everything others do or say is some kind of direct, personal reaction to the person. We also compare ourselves to others, trying to determine who is smarter, better looking, etc. A person engaging in personalization may also see themselves as the cause of some unhealthy external event that they were not responsible for. For example, "We were late to the dinner party and that caused the hostess to overcook the meal. If I had only pushed my husband to leave on time, this wouldn't have happened."

7. Control Fallacies.

If we feel *externally controlled*, we see ourselves as helpless a victim of fate. For example, "I can't help it if the quality of the work is poor; my boss demanded I work overtime on it." The fallacy of internal control has us assuming responsibility for the pain and happiness of everyone around us. For example, "Why aren't you happy? Is it because of something I did?"

8. Fallacy of Fairness.

We feel resentful because we think we know what is fair, but other people won't agree with us. As our parents tell us when we're growing up and something doesn't go our way, "Life isn't always fair." People who go through life applying a measuring ruler against every situation judging its "fairness" will often feel badly and negative because of it. Because life isn't "fair", things will not always work out in your favor, even when you think they should.

9. Blaming.

We hold other people responsible for our pain, or take the other track and blame ourselves for every problem. For example, "Stop making me feel bad about myself!" Nobody can "make" us feel any particular way, only we have control over our own emotions and emotional reactions.

10. Should.

We have a list of ironclad rules about how others and we *should* behave. People who break the rules make us angry, and we feel guilty when we violate these rules. A person may often believe they are trying to motivate themselves with shoulds and *shouldn'ts*, as if they have to be punished before they can do anything. For example, "I really should exercise. I shouldn't be so lazy." Musts and oughts are also offenders. The emotional consequence is guilt. When a person directs *should statements* toward others, they often feel anger, frustration and resentment.

It should be noted that it takes effort and a lot of practice to help the client reframe deeply ingrained thinking patterns. The goal is to refute the negative thinking over and over slowly diminishing over time, replaced by more rational and balanced thinking. Grohol (2009) continues in *Fixing Cognitive Distortions* by listing several steps to help correct cognitive distortions.

1. Identify Cognitive Distortion

Create a list of troublesome thoughts and examine them later for matches with a list of cognitive distortions.

2. Examine the Evidence.

A thorough examination of an experience allows us to identify the basis for our distorted thoughts. If we are quite self-critical, then, we should identify a number of experiences and situations where we had success.

3. Double Standard Method.

An alternative to "self-talk" that is harsh and demeaning is to talk to ourselves in the same compassionate and caring way that we would talk with a friend in a similar situation.

4. Thinking in Shades of Gray.

Instead of thinking about our problem or predicament in an either-or polarity, evaluate things on a scale of 0-100. When a plan or goal is not fully realized, think about and evaluate the experience as a partial success, again, on a scale of 0-100.

5. Survey Method.

We need to seek the opinions of others regarding whether our thoughts and attitudes are realistic. If we believe that our anxiety about an upcoming event is unwarranted, check with a few trusted friends or relatives.

6. Definitions.

What does it mean to define ourselves as "inferior," "a loser," "a fool," or "abnormal." An examination of these and other global labels likely will reveal that they more closely represent specific behaviors, or an identifiable behavior pattern instead of the total person.

7. Re-attribution.

Often, we automatically blame ourselves for the problems and predicaments we experience. Identify external factors and other individuals that contributed to the problem. Regardless of the degree of responsibility we assume, our energy is best utilized in the pursuit of resolutions to problems or identifying ways to cope with predicaments.

8. Cost-Benefit Analysis.

It is helpful to list the advantages and disadvantages of feelings, thoughts, or behaviors. A cost-benefit analysis will help us to ascertain what we are gaining from feeling bad, distorted thinking, and inappropriate behavior.

MI Principles to Use in the Assessment Process

As previously mentioned, MI is a style of interacting with clients, not something you do one time (Mid-Atlantic Addiction Technology Transfer Center, 2013). The following four principles guide the practice of MI throughout treatment:

Expressing empathy relies on the client perceiving the coach as able to see the world as the client sees it. The important point with empathy is that the clientbelieves the coach is able to understand and feel the way the client does. It does not mean that the coach has gone through exactly what the client has, only that the client feels able to be heard and understood. Empathy serves as the foundation of trust in the relationship and the client is more likelyto be honest with the coach.

Supporting self-efficacy is the way the coach encourages the client to build on their strengths and resources in order to believe that change is possible.

Rolling with resistanceis usually the most difficult principle to get used to, but the goal is to eliminate confrontation with the client and guide them to come to terms with their own desire to change. It includes de-escalation of conflict, not challenging a client's ambivalence and "dancing" rather than "wrestling" with a client's desire to change.

Developing discrepancy is showing clients the mismatches between where they are and where they say they want to be. The goal is to guide the clients to the recognition that their current situation is interfering with their goals. Clients eventually become aware that their current behaviors are leading them away from what they want.

MI Skills

The next question becomes, "How is this done?" The goal is to guide clients to positive change talk and generating their own commitment to change. OARS is a set of skills used to elicit change talk using the principle listed above.

Open-ended questions are those questions which require more than a "yes/no" or short, specific answer. Open-ended questions invite elaboration and deep thinking creating the momentum needed for clients to explore the possibility of change. An example would be, "Tell me about the time you were successful quitting for a short time."

Affirmations are the key to supporting self-efficacy and helps clients see themselves in a positive light. Often, clients are blind to their strengths in early recovery and may not view certain behaviors as positive. Continuing with the open-ended question above, the client may say they got a new job that was intellectually challenging and only went back to using because the company downsized and they got bored. You could respond to the client by telling them that taking on a difficult job like that took a lot of tenacity and determination and perhaps that intellectual curiosity is the key to staying clean.

Reflections or reflective listening is a crucial helping skill that helps a client feel understood and builds empathy. It involves understanding what a client is saying and then offering it back to the client to confirm that understanding. An example of a reflection, using the example above, could be: "You must have been devastated when the company down-sized."

Summaries are a type of reflection that recaps what the clients concerns are and can highlight both sides of a client's ambivalence as well as promote the development of discrepancy by strategically selecting what is included and not included in thesummary. For example, "You have been able to quit on your own, cold turkey, without treatment when you were in an environment that supported your natural intellectual curiosity, but when something out of your control took that away, you felt helpless and lapsed."

Keep in mind that this is a basic overview of Motivational Interviewing and that training is available to develop these skills to proficiency. If you are able to integrate MI into every aspect of your client relationships, you will find clients will trust you quicker, will generate their own change talk faster, and recovery outcomes will be more positive.

Suggested assessments

There are many types of formal assessments available and as a coach gains more experience, assessment will become a more fluid, informal, integrated part of getting to know a client. Assessments that are more formalized are helpful for a number of reasons, mostly for establishing a starting point from which to measure progress.

History of substance use and current use

Obtaining a history of substance use in the initial meeting is most important if you are the first point of contact. If you are not, save time and frustration by getting historical information from the client's treatment provider so you can focus on the client's current situation.

Information to gather in a substance use history includes:

- Each substance used
- First use & amount used for each substance
- Last use & amount used for each substance
- Typical pattern of use for each substance
- Evaluate tolerance for each substance. Has the client used more and for a longer period than intended?
- Has the client had persistent desire and unsuccessful attempts to quit and cut down?
- Has the client spent excessive amounts of time using, obtaining, and recovering from the effects of the substance?
- Has the client continued use despite social problems caused or exacerbated by use
- What stage of change is the client in for each substance?

Mental health history-check for co-occurring disorders and suicidality

Due to the prevalence of co-occurring disorders, it's important to screen substance use clients for mental health and suicidal ideation. This can be done in an informal interview, or in a more formal manner by having a client fill out a questionnaire themselves. The Modified Mini Screen (MMS) (Hazelden Foundation, 2013) in the appendix has basic questions to alert you if a client should be evaluated further. This screen can be used to address safety in the case of suicidal ideation, to discover potential mental health causes for substance use, and to refer a client to a mental health professional. The MMS has a question for suicidal ideation, but it's important to assess risk yourself. Clients with a history of substance use are likely to have a history of trauma, all of which are risk factors for self-harm. A brief suicide risk assessment form is included in the appendix.

Stages of Change – Client centered inspiration for change

Recovery, like any major life change, is a difficult journey that is not always successful the first time around. The stages of change model of recovery is a spiral, taking relapse into account, and allowing for success despite setbacks (Connors, Donovan & DiClemente, 2001). This model stresses meeting a client where they are in their process of change and using motivational interviewing will help a client to come to their own decisions about change through stage appropriate interventions.

TABLE 1.1. Stages of Change and Associated Features

Stage of change	Main characteristics of individuals in this stage	Intervention match	To move to next stage
Precontemplation	• No intent to change • Problem behavior seen as having more pros than cons	• Do *not* focus on behavioral change • Use motivational strategies	• Acknowledge problem • Increase awareness of negatives of problem • Evaluate self-regulatory activities
Contemplation	• Thinking about changing • Seeking information about problem • Evaluating pros and cons of change • Not prepared to change yet	• Consciousness raising • Self-reevaluation • Environmental reevaluation	• Make decision to act • Engage in preliminary action
Preparation	• Ready to change in attitude and behavior • May have begun to increase self-regulation and to change	• Same as contemplation • Increase commitment or self-liberation	• Set goals and priorities to achieve change • Develop change plan
Action	• Modifying the problem behavior • Learning skills to prevent reversal to full return to problem behavior	• Methods of overt behavior change • Behavioral change processes	• Apply behavior change methods for average of 6 months • Increase self-efficacy to perform the behavior change
Maintenance	• Sustaining changes that have been accomplished	• Methods of overt behavior change continued	

Note. Data from Prochaska and DiClemente (1983, 1992).

Many substance abuse treatment facilities and mental health facilities use stages of change to drive level of care placement criteria, treatment planning and evaluation. Understanding what stages your client is in will help you coordinate treatment and guide your client through recovery at their pace.

Keep in mind that a client will have more than one stage of change. For example, your client has been using alcohol and methamphetamine for 5 years and wants to quit drinking because of a recent liver disorder diagnosis. The client works full time and loves his job. He talks about getting and using meth with his coworkers who happen to be his best friends and says meth makes him a better worker. His manager, however, has given him a warning about aggressive behavior displays at work. He has no other friends outside of work and often drinks when he's alone so he doesn't have to think. Although it's been difficult for him, he has changed his drinking habits from every night after work to one night on the weekend. He has also started eating healthy and exercising upon the recommendation of his doctor.

Applying the stages of change to this example may look like this:

Problem	Stage of change
Alcohol abuse	preparation
Methamphetamine abuse	precontemplation
Physical health problems	action
Trouble at work	precontemplation
Friends who use	precontemplation

Once you have the stages of change for each problem, it becomes easier to prioritize a recovery plan. In this example, the client has already demonstrated that his health is important to him by the actions he's taken since his liver diagnosis. Interventions stressing the physical effects of methamphetamines and educating the client about health dangers taps into the client's values, increasing the probability of moving the client out of the precontemplation stage. As problem areas are targeted and the client moves through each stage, progress is also easily demonstrated.

MBTI – Self-discovery

The official Myers-Briggs Type Indicator is a continuum based personality inventory that measures preferences as opposed to traits, abilities, and character. Only qualified trainers can administer and interpret the full MBTI, but those interested in a shorter, self-help version can go to www.humanmetrics.com to take the Jung Typology Test which is the basis of the MBTI. Here, a client can get their 4 letter type to gain insight on their preferences.

How could this be helpful to a recovery coach and the client?

- Increases self-awareness

- Affirms things clients may already know about themselves ("So that's why I don't like crowds!")

- Gives the client permission to explore their identity and potential strengths.

- A recovery coach can suggest healthy lifestyle changes in congruence with the client's preferences. For example, an extreme introvert who doesn't like sharing feelings will have a hard time sharing at a 12-step meeting and a coach can provide other options.

The General Self Efficacy Scale – Empowerment

According to Social Cognitive Theory the prime factor that influences behavior is self-efficacy, which is defined as a person's belief in their ability to achieve an intended goal (Killeen, 2013). It also is defined as having the ability to cope with a broad range of stressful or challenging demands, both of which are common during the recovery process.

The General Self-Efficacy Scale gets a client thinking about their own self-efficacy, gives the coach insight, and provides ideas for areas of improvement. Taken at the beginning of recovery and after a time in recovery can show a client how they are changing and building self-efficacy.

Strengths, Grit, and Optimism – Tapping client resources

The Authentic Happiness Center at the University of Pennsylvania is the culmination of the work of positive psychologist Martin E.P. Seligman. His theories of happiness and resilience is based upon the belief that people have the ability to make change in their lives and flourish if they pay attention to and use the strengths and resources they already possess. The Center's website has a number of questionnaires clients can use to learn about the positive aspects of themselves. Three that can be helpful in recovery coaching is the Brief Strengths Test, The Grit Survey, and the Optimism Test. The strengths test can help you guide a client towards internal resources they may not be aware they possess, the measure of grit complements the self-efficacy scale by measuring how the client may respond to future adversities (i.e. relapse), and the optimism test can tell you how the client views the upcoming recovery journey. Again, using these assessments later in recovery can show the client measurable progress.

Coping Assessment – Identification of coping skills

A final assessment that can be helpful for clients and coaches is an evaluation of current coping skills a client uses when stressed. Often, a substance has been the client's coping mechanism and when that is taken away in recovery, the safety and security of that coping mechanism is also gone. The goal is to help the client find healthier coping mechanisms to replace unhealthy ones. The Brief COPE questionnaire categorizes skills into emotion-focused, problem-focused, and dysfunctional skills. The list of skills not only provides identification of current skills, but it also helps drive conversation about the types of skills the client would like to develop. From here, goals for learning new skills can be written for the recovery plan and retaking the questionnaire further in recovery will show measurable results of progress.

RECOVERY PLANNING

Background

- **Using Assessments**
- **Recovery Plans**
- **Recovery Capital**
- **Relapse Prevention**

Using Assessments

The initial assessment phase will provide you with a lot of information about your client and will guide your next steps, but assessment will be ongoing throughout recovery. The substance use history, mental health screen and suicide assessments will help you determine if the client needs additional help and will support your referrals to other agencies and providers. The stages of change will help you and your client determine goals for recovery and the assessments of self (MBTI, General Self-Efficacy, Strengths, Grit, Optimism, and Brief COPE) will show the client resources and recovery capital available to achieve their goals.

Taking the client through assessment, goal setting, and progress evaluations, you are also modeling positive life skills that your client can put to use. Through your example, they will learn to identify challenges, identify and tap resources to meet the challenges, and revise upon evaluation if necessary.

SMART Goals

Goals provide clients with a way to plan for what they want in recovery and give them benchmarks to celebrate progress. Research suggests that those who write and formulate specific, measurable, achievable, realistic and time-bound (SMART) goals are more likely to achieve them (Meyer, 2003).

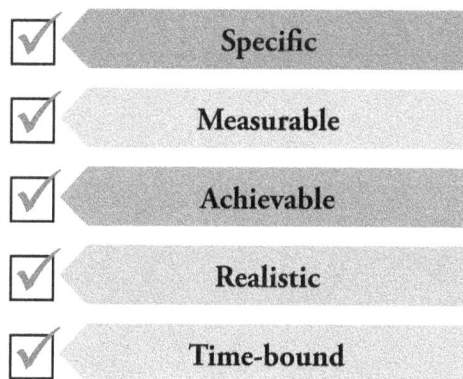

☑ **Specific**

☑ **Measurable**

☑ **Achievable**

☑ **Realistic**

☑ **Time-bound**

SMART goals are specific and strategic. For example, it is not enough to state "I want a job."A coach would guide a client through questions (Who? What? Where? When?)to further define what this means to them. A more specific goal would be: "I want a job as a nurse'said at a major metropolitan hospital."

Secondly, SMART goals are measurable. This ensures that there is a way to measure progress towards the goal. Not only does this help the client stay on track towards their goals, but agencies, treatment centers and payers like Medicare or health insurance companies will require that goals are documented with a concrete criterion in place. Without a goal being measureable, there is no way to determine if a client has achieved their goal. Returning to the job example, it could be made measurable by adding "by applying for 2 positions per week."

The goal must also be attainable and achievable. We want to be sure that we are setting the client up for success, so a goal should be within reach. Does the client have the skills, knowledge and resources to obtain the goal?If a client has no training to become a nurse's aid, the goal might be rewritten to include the pursuit of training. "Take 2 year training course at the community college."

Goals also need to be realistic.For example, some professions that require licensing or certification, such as those in healthcare, may have restrictions related to legal history and certain forms of substance use. If your client has a felony possession of opiates charge on their record, it may be extremely difficult for them to be considered for licensure. It may be appropriate, however, to add researching certification requirements to the goal to determine whether the goal is realistic.

Finally, goals must be time bound. Again agencies, treatment centers and payers, like state funders, Medicare or health insurance companies, will also require a time frame for goals and often these goals will be established around a voucher, a waiver and/or review period. For example, a common review period is 90 days. A sample goal with a time frame might be "apply for nurse's aid training program within 30 days and start classes within 60 days." Giving a goal a time frame allows you to reflect back on progress and determine if your client has reached the goal.

Wheel of Life

The Wheel of Life, also referred to as the Life Balance Circle, can help clients formulate goals by giving them a visual representation of their current life situation and determine if there is a balance within their life (MindTools, 2013). By examining each area, the client and coach can identify what areas are off balance and which areas might need more of the client's time and attention. There are eight main aspects of life that are identified on the wheel.

- Finances
- Friends and Family
- Fun and Recreation
- Career or Business
- Romance
- Personal Growth
- Physical Environment
- Health and Wellness

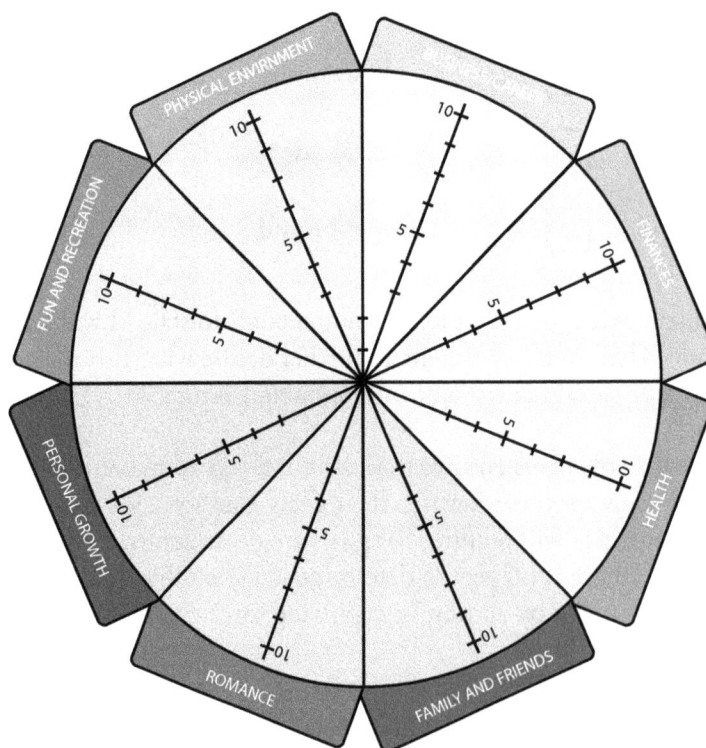

The Wheel of Life®. Reproduced with permission from Mind Tools.

A recovery coach can guide a client through each component of the wheel. The center of the wheel is marked as 0 representing the lowest satisfaction level. The edge of each component is marked as 10, representing the highest level of satisfaction.

The scoring is as follows:

0-4 means they are not satisfied
5-7 means they are more or less satisfied, but further attention should be sought
8-10 means there is a high level of satisfaction

Once a client has marked each of the components, a line will be drawn to connect the marks around the wheel. This will give the client and the coach a visual representation of how balanced their life is, and shows the client what areas need improvement. The areas that received low scores are those that may need more attention. To further process the Wheel of Life tool results, the recovery coach can help the client identify the lowest satisfaction level areas (those with the lowest numerical score) and prepare an action plan with SMART goals on how to achieve balance. For example you might ask the client "What would make you more satisfied with this area of your life?" Then to build on their response you could ask "What are the specific steps that you could take to ensure satisfaction in this area?" Having the client write these steps down is a powerful tool. It is suggested that the client write these steps down directly on their Wheel of Life and keep it. Then at a later date the client can complete the same process to see if their life is more or less balanced by comparing the results.

Another technique for using this tool is through the use of a blank Wheel of Life which allows the client to personalize their own components.

1. Start by brainstorming with the client to select the eight outside dimensions of the circles. These dimensions are the aspects of the client's life that are important for them. Different suggestions for these dimensions are:
   – The roles played in life for example: husband/wife, father/mother, manager, colleague, team member, sports player, community leader, or friend
   – Areas of life that are important for example: recovery, artistic expression, positive attitude, career, education, family, friends, spirituality, financial freedom, physical challenge, pleasure, or public service
2. Any combination of these (or different) things reflect the things that are your client's priorities in life. (e.g. family, friends, work, health, fun and recreation). Describe this approach assuming what will help the coaching client be happy and fulfilled if they could find the right balance of attention for each of these aspects of their lives. Also understand that different areas of the client's life will need different levels of attention at different times. Write down these dimensions on the Blank Wheel of Life diagram, in the area on the outer ring of each spoke of the life wheel in the boxes provided
3. Begin by asking the client questions linked to the current dimension of their life to complete this portion. An example question may be: "Are your priorities in life focused around your family?" Considering each current dimension or area in turn, the low scale would be 1, meaning totally avoiding that aspect of life; the high scale is 5 representing giving that dimension of their life a lot of attention, receiving satisfaction and a sense of achievement. Have the client place a dot on the spoke of the wheel to designate the numerical amount that they have achieved in that area of their life. An example could be in the area of finances, a statement saying "I am gaining control of my finances". This statement could produce a 3 or 4 on the Wheel. On the Blank Wheel of Life mark a dot between 3 and 4 on the spoke for the dimension of finances. Follow this same procedure around the wheel. Then, connect the dot-marks around the circle. Have the client look at the Life Wheel and see if the Life Wheel confirms how much attention they are giving to certain areas of their life, currently.

4. Next it's time to consider the ideal level in each area of their life. A balanced life does not mean getting a 5 in each life dimension/area: Naturally, some areas may need more attention and focus than others at any time (e.g. children need more focus than house maintenance). Inevitably, the client will need to make choices and compromises, as their time and energy are not in unlimited supply! So the question is what would the ideal level of attention be for them in each life area? Plot the "ideal" scores around the Life Wheel, using a different colored pen or marker to indicate the client's ideal goals in which to work towards for a more balanced life.

5. Now connect the dots-marks, using the same colored pen that was used for the ideal areas. Now the coaching client has a visual representation of their current life balance and ideal life balance. This is an opportunity to examine the gaps. Gaps are the areas of the client's life that need attention. Remember that gaps can go both ways. Gaps are indicated on the wheel by open spaces between the two different colored plot lines around the circle. There are certain areas that are not getting as much attention as the coach or the client would like.

However, there may also be areas where the client is putting in more effort than they should. These areas are sapping the client's energy and enthusiasm that may better be directed elsewhere.

6. Once the client has identified the areas that need attention, it's time to plan the actions needed to work on regaining balance. Starting with the neglected areas, the areas of 1's and 2's, what does the client need to start doing to regain balance? In the areas that currently sap their energy and time, what can they stop doing, reprioritize or delegate to someone else? Allow the client to make a commitment to these actions by writing them in a daily journal.

Recovery Plans

Once assessments are completed and goals formulated, the recovery plan is developed. If assessments give a client's current picture and goals are where the client wants to go, the recovery plan is the map to get there. Not only will the plan guide the client towards their goals, but it will also help the client identifyand cultivate internal and external resources they will need for successful recovery.

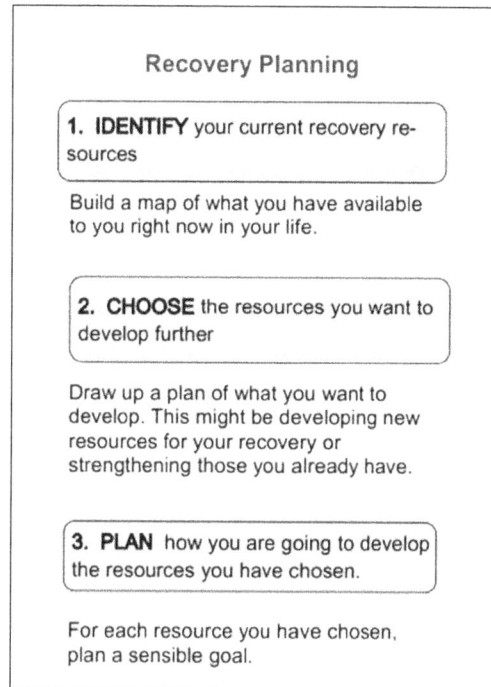

Recovery Planning

> **1. IDENTIFY** your current recovery re-sources
>
> Build a map of what you have available to you right now in your life.
>
> **2. CHOOSE** the resources you want to develop further
>
> Draw up a plan of what you want to develop. This might be developing new resources for your recovery or strengthening those you already have.
>
> **3. PLAN** how you are going to develop the resources you have chosen.
>
> For each resource you have chosen, plan a sensible goal.

(Torbay& Southern Devon Health & Care, 2013)

GROW Recovery Plans

There are several frameworks to help structure your recovery plan, but one that works well for structuring a coaching discussion is the GROW model (Killeen, 2013). It was originally developed by a performance coach with the coach acting as a facilitator; helping the client select the best options rather than offering advice or direction.

1. **G**oals, establishing goals through the use of various instruments (can be used with SMART goals)
2. **R**eality, compare the reality of the situation
3. **O**ptions, explore the client's options
4. **W**rap up or Write the Recovery Plan

The first step is the formulation of goals and can be combined with the SMART goals and the Wheel of Life exercises.

Secondly, the coach will compare the reality of the client's situation in relation to their goal, reality represents the "R" in GROW. The purpose here is for there to be an accurate assessment of where the client currently is, in relation to their goals and where they want to be. If the goals are not realistic, the recovery coach can help shape the client goals to ensure that they are realistic and reachable.

The "O" in GROW represents the clients current options. The goal is not to find a solution immediately, but to generate several possible alternatives by brainstorming potential courses of action. Once several options have been identified, the recovery coach and client can work to select one option to put into action.

The final step is often referred to as "wrap up" and also "way forward," but it is also the point where the recovery coach begins "writing" the recovery plan. This is where the discussion is put into action and the client begins to take the actions needed to move forward towards their goals.

Strengths Based Recovery Plans

The strengths based approach focuses on the client's strengths and makes them the focus of building resources. Clients are asked to identify their personal strengths, abilities, achievements and personal qualities. This allows clients to have a voice in their treatment while developing independence and empowerment. Hammond (2010) states that this strength-based approach offers a different language to describe difficulties and struggles since the starting point is "what's right with person." It allows one to see opportunities, avoids labeling, and casts the coach as a partner rather than as an expert. A defining feature of this approach is that it believes that everyone has the potential to learn, grow and change. Considering a client's strengths can be a coach's overall philosophy in addition to a model for developing recovery plans.

The 5 principles of the strength based approach include:

1. The focus is on individual strengths rather than the addiction (pathology).
2. The community is viewed as an oasis of resources.
3. Interventions are based on the needs and desires of the client (self-determination).
4. Aggressive, recovery community outreach is the preferred model of intervention.
5. People suffering from addiction can continue to learn, grow and change.

"Assessing strengths requires a focus on capacities to move forward in the face of adversity, using positive learning experiences and rewarding success" (Killeen, 2013). While clients may struggle to focus on their strengths, the role of the recovery coach is to help the client identify their past successes and current strengths. This approach is used throughout the treatment relationship with the client's strengths being used to help them reach their goals.

Recovery Capital

Recovery capital (RC) is defined as the breadth and depth of internal and external resources that can be drawn upon to initiate and sustain recovery (White & Cloud, 2008) as well as the quality of the client's life, their home or family life, the status of their work life, their financial security and their physical or mental health (Killeen, 2013).

William White & Dr. William Cloud (2008) identify three types of recovery capital; personal, family/social and community recovery capital which are to be the focus of every recovery coach.

Personal recovery capital can be divided into physical and human capital. A client's physical recovery capital includes physical health, financial assets, health insurance, shelter, clothing, food, and access to transportation. Within this group is a sub group of Human recovery capital, which includes a client's values, knowledge, educational/vocational skills and/or credentials. It also includes their problem solving capacities, self-awareness, self-esteem, and self-efficacy (which is defined as the self-confidence in managing high risk situations). Personal recovery capital also includes hopefulness, optimism, the perception of one's past/present/future, a sense of meaning or purpose in life, and the client's interpersonal skills.

Family and social recovery capital is indicated by the willingness of friends, intimate partners and family members to participate in understanding treatment and recovery. It includes the presence of others in recovery, both within the family and the client's social network. It assures access to sober outlets for sobriety-based fellowship, leisure activities, and relational connections to conventional institutions (school, workplace, church, and other mainstream community organizations).

Community recovery capital encompasses community attitudes/policies/resources related to addiction and recovery that promote the resolution of alcohol and other drug abuse problems. Does your client's community include these signs of Community Recovery Capital? Are active efforts made to reduce addiction/recovery-related stigmas in the community? Is there a visible and diverse local presence of a variety of recovery role models, and a full continuum of addiction treatment resources in the client's neighborhood? Are resources of 12 step or mutual aid meetings that are accessible within a local recovery community, and which can include recovery support centers or other social services? Are the accessible services that provide resources of sustained recovery support, early intervention and social services, for example health care, welfare and food stamps?

Developing recovery capital is part of a long term, approach to recovery from substance abuse and is aimed at preventing relapse. Recovery capital should be assessed both at the time of assessment and frequently during the coaching relationship. Many times clients will enter a treatment center with great recovery capital (good finances, strong family support, steady job, etc.) but when leaving treatment these resources will be depleted. An addict leaving treatment may not have a home or job to return to (Killeen, 2013). If it is determined that a client has poor recovery capital upon discharge this can be an additional stress on the client. This added stress could result in a relapse. This is important to note since research has demonstrated that relapse is highest during the earliest stages of recovery, a recovery coach would want to ensure that developing recovery capital is a high priority (Laudet& William, 2008).

A tool to measure recovery capital is the Recovery Capital Scale (White & Cloud, 1998). It is designed as a self-assessment tool and can be completed by the client and then discussed together at the initial interview. The Recovery Capital Scale uses the Likert scale in which a client will assign a 1-5 numerical score to each question that ranges from strongly agree to strongly disagree.

After assessing recovery capital the recovery coach will be able to determine the client's recovery capital strengths and weaknesses. The coach can help identify the gaps of what might be missing. This is a very individualized method and there is no "one size fits all" approach. Each client will be different and should be treated as a unique individual.

A client may have very little or zero recovery capital at discharge from a treatment center. This will need to be rebuilt and may begin with basic skills, like hygiene, or wellness skills as well as educational, and/or career coaching. Rebuilding the client's recovery capital is a vital step in recovery and can be done by locating resources for housing, coordinating transportation, and job assistance (Killeen, 2013). This course of coaching would vary since "every person's recovery capital is different because each of us has different resources available to use in our lives" (Torbay& Southern Devon Health & Care, 2013). Granfield and Cloud (1999) go further to state that recovery capital differs within the same individual at multiple points in their life.

In addition a client's level of severity should be taken into consideration. A client with a severe problem but very high recovery capital may require fewer resources to initiate and sustain recovery than an individual with a less severe problem but very low recovery capital (Granfield& Cloud, 1999). For example, a client with high recovery capital might do well in outpatient counseling, link to recovery support groups and need a moderate level of ongoing monitoring, while a client with a low level of recovery capital may require a higher intensity of treatment, greater enmeshment in a culture of recovery (e.g., placement in a long term recovery home or ½ way house, greater intensity of support group or outpatient treatment involvement, involvement in recovery-based social activities), and a more demanding level of supervision by the recovery coach.

Relapse Prevention

WRAP®

Mary Ellen Copeland, an internationally acclaimed author, educator, and mental health advocate, initially developed the Wellness Recovery Action Plan®, or WRAP® to help with her own struggles with mental health challenges (Copeland, 2012) Research supports that people with mental health and substance abuse disorders have been able to self- manage their conditions with positive outcomes using this approach. Currently WRAP® is being utilized in formal and informal recovery programs in all 50 U.S. States and in countries around the world. WRAP® has been recognized as an Evidence Based Practice in the field of mental health recovery.

Even though relapse is part of recovery, a good recovery coach can identify when their client is coming close to the "slippery slope" by using the WRAP® method. This information can be developed with the client after they create their recovery plan and sobriety has started to take hold. Relapse, even if expected, can move to crisis very quickly. As described by people in recovery, "addiction" has been doing "push-ups in the parking lot" and returns even stronger than it was before the client became sober. There are many stories of individuals thinking, "I'll try this just once," and end up on a binge that lasts a week, or worse, dead from an overdose (Killeen, 2013).

Just as emergency planning works in a natural disaster, the WRAP® method of relapse planning works for the addict/alcoholic to prevent relapse. It is imperative that your client completes a Relapse Prevention Plan (or Action Plan as the WRAP® guidelines call it) when sober, while the client has a reasonable amount of clear headedness under their belt to formulate the plan (Killeen, 2013).

The WRAP® method involves your client listing their personal resources, called Wellness Tools, and then using the following guidelines to develop an Action Plan to use in specific situations in which they need extra support in maintaining their sobriety. WRAP® also includes a Crisis Plan or Advance Directive which is helpful in the event the addict cannot make decisions on their intervention because of a relapse, such as if the client is unconscious from an over dose, or an auto accident. The Wellness Recovery Action Plan© encourages your client to create a list for the following categories:

1. Wellness Tools-Things that keep me well

2. A Daily Maintenance Plan-What keeps me well

3. Triggers – What do I have to watch out for

4. Triggers Action Plan-What do I do when I am triggered?

5. Early Warning Signs –What are my early warning signs of relapse?

6. Early Warning Signs Action Plan- What must I do, who will I ask for help?

7. This is How I KnowWhen Things are Breaking Down - Things are going downhill fast, what am I doing?

8. Relapse Action Plan – This is what I have to do when I relapse

9. Crisis Plan or Advance Directive – This is what I want to be done, in the event my relapse leaves me unable to speak for myself

10. Post Crisis Plan. –OK, its' over, where do I go from here? What have I learned?

11. What do I revise in the Action Plan?

SUPPORTING ACTIVITIES

Background

- **Self-Advocacy**
- **Accessing Programs**
- **Finding a Job**

Self-Advocacy

Self-advocacy is often thought of as speaking up for oneself, although it is much more than that. As a recovery coach, you will want to be sure that you are helping your client develop the ability to advocate for themselves. According to research, allowing a client to help themselves and make their own choices allows them to take charge of their life more fully and develops a greater sense of self confidence (National Alliance on Mental Illness, 2013). This develops empowerment which can be defined as self-advocacy, and can be accomplished by training the client to act on their own behalf and empowering the client to change their environment directly so that their rights and entitlements are protected (Rothman, & Sager, 1998). This approach also allows the client to take responsibility for their life, while you act as a support system. Self-advocacy would also include demanding respect from others, making your own decisions, and standing up for your rights.

As a recovery coach you want to make sure that your client is aware of these rights. These include, but are not limited to the following:

- Ask for what you want
- Say yes or no
- Change your mind
- Make mistakes
- Follow your own values, standards and spiritual beliefs throughout treatment
- Express your feelings
- Determine what is important to you
- Make your own decisions based on what you need
- Be treated with dignity, compassion and respect at all times
- Decide on services and supports that are right for you and lead you on the path to recovery
- Be listened to
- Be aware of all treatment options
- Have time to make decisions
- Be encouraged
- Communicate your concerns, symptoms and thoughts
- Involve friends and family in the treatment progress when applicable
- Be yourself
- Be safe
- Ask for a second opinion
- Express concerns and ask questions
- Be taught how to help yourself
- Receive as much information as possible about the risks and benefits of all treatment options, including anticipated outcomes
- Weigh the pros and cons of recommended treatments
- Track and evaluate your progress, symptoms and outcomes.

Clients, may shrink from this role and instead of confrontation will try to use collaboration, cooperation, and discussion tactics (Rothman, & Sager, 1998). While collaboration, cooperation and discussion can be utilized initially, if the desired resolution is not reached, the recovery coach can assist the client in the advocacy process. Research demonstrates that positive outcomes are associated with the use of communication and mediation rather than power.

The value and application of self-advocacy is illustrated as follows:

One of my clients was upset about the way a residential monitor had treated her while she was at detox. When the client arrived in my office in the morning she told me that she should report the residential monitor and took the step of taking the monitor's name down. I encouraged her to go ahead with her request and made my office phone available. By being near her, I provided support, but not offer direct assistance. After reporting what had occurred to the director of the detox center, the client discussed with me how she felt. She felt so much better and was proud of herself. Clearly she had developed a new skill to aid in her recovery.

Your work as a recovery coach is to help the client find their voice through the recovery process. Self-advocacy is a skill that is needed throughout the recovery process, although there are often specific events that can trigger the need for advocacy services. Typically, advocacy services are needed when a client is denied social services such as food stamps or welfare, but may also occur when there is an imbalance of power and resources (Rothman, & Sager, 1998). The goal of self-advocacy would be to resolve the conflict at hand, which in this case would mean the client reporting the inappropriate behavior of a monitor. Research by Bartlett (1986), demonstrates that it is necessary for clients to develop the following advocacy competencies:

- General advocacy skills and strategies, e.g., developing effective personal relations, developing knowledge, self-confidence, and savvy listening and negotiating skills;
- Preparation skills and strategies, e.g./ gaining access to administration, setting reasonable goals, and learning the rules of the game;
- Implementation skills and strategies, e.g., being concrete in explaining patient education, establishing quality assurance policies, and persistence.

Accessing Programs

During the assessment process, clients will go through the Wheel of Life exercise. That wheel has several dimensions in it that are outside the scope of what a recovery coach can provide. As a coach, you are expected to guide the client through building resources, acting as a hub of sorts to help clients build self-efficacy and make connections.Clients in recovery are often intimidated by the perceived difficulty in making drastic lifestyle changes. One of the most effective ways a coach can help is through modeling and introducing clients to recovery-oriented services.

For example, a coach may have a relationship with the local workforce development agency where clients can be introduced to case workers with whom the coach has a relationship. Those relationships benefit the client in several ways including reducing anxiety related to the unknown entity. Ifall parties are educated about the process of recovery, the stigma of a substance using history can be less of a barrier and conversation about the type of work or work environment for which the client is best suited becomes easier. Should problems arise during the process, the coach can also help with proactive solutions designed to help the client maintain recovery.

Healthy and social life are two other areas on the wheel of life for which a coach may be helpful. Perhaps the coach has a relationship with a doctor's office that provides general health care, but has knowledge and empathy about the physical consequences of substance use. For some clients, it can be difficult to re-establish relationships with physicians, especially if the client was known as a "med-seeker." The coach can act as a bridge and a support to both the client and the physician. For example, if the physician notices a client's behavior changing or reverting to old behaviors, the coach can be invited to participate and support the client.

For many clients, using was their social life and transitioning to "sober life" can be a daunting task. A coach can serve as a source of information about recovery-oriented events, groups or organizations that promote healthy living. These groups do not need to be recovery-specific, but may emphasize outdoor activities, physical fitness or other healthy lifestyle activities that can be used to replace unhealthy activities.

A client may also need to access local, state or county social services such as signing up for disability, accessing health insurance, securing an attorney, navigating through family services or the judicial process. Partof the role of the recovery coach is to identify the need for services and help the client locate and access them. If a coach has knowledge about the services available, the coach can guide the client to help when and if it is needed. It is recommended that a coach has access to those services and knows about the basic eligibility requirements for them. As with the other aspects of recovery mentioned above, it is best if the coach has relationships established with social service agencies and organizations to facilitate introductions.

Finding a Job

This is an exciting time since the role of a recovery coach is becoming more widely accepted and valued. The Department of Veteran Affairs (VA) has trained and hired peer specialists in mass numbers. "In some ways, the VA's efforts have encouraged states that once considered peer support meaningless or marginally meaningful to reconsider their positions and, ultimately, create peer specialist programs" (Harrington, 2011).

In 2001, Georgia became the first state to obtain Medicaid reimbursement for peer support services (such as a recovery coaches) and since then, 13 other states have followed suit (Harrington, 2011). With the growing demand for recovery services, the peer support specialist profession will enjoy considerable (and likely rapid) growth in the next decade. One recent study has shown that peer support can reduce re-hospitalization by as much as 72 percent (OptumHealth.com, 2011).

Some of the factors driving this increase include the following:

- The growing recognition of the reality of recovery from severe and persistent psychiatric conditions
- A political climate that expects cost-effectiveness for public funds
- Positive outcomes associated with peer support
- A ready labor force
- The establishment of formal peer training and certification of peer specialists (Harrington, 2011).

There are many associations for recovery coaches or peer support specialists including the National Association of Peer Specialists (NAPS), Recovery Coaches International (RCI), the International Coaching Federation (ICF). In addition to the national organizations, check your state for resources and continue networking through PARfessionals.

Certification still varies and each state has their own requirements. Contact your state credentialing bureau or your state's licensing department to find out the requirements for certification as a recovery coach. Some states require training only, while others require a number of supervised hours of work or volunteer coaching experience. Some states require the completion of a comprehensive exam, request references, an interview, background investigations or a combination of all of these. One of the largest certification organizations that features a peer mentoring credential is the IC&RC (2013). This Harrisburg, PA, based organization offers certification credentials that are recognized by all fifty states.

The outlook looks great, but you still might be asking yourself what does it take to become a recovery coach running your own business? According to Killeen (2013), one must have an entrepreneurial mindsetand strategic information on the business structure of recovery coaching and support. If you decide to become a recovery coach on your own rather than working for an organization, strong business skills will help you to succeed.

You will want to register your business with the IRS and obtain a tax identification number. Killeen (2013), also suggests employing a good accountant, a business attorney, and becoming familiar with computer programs for small businesses such as Quicken or Peachtree. Obtaining liability and malpracticeinsurance to protect you and your business is also essential.Marketing is an important role for the entrepreneur and this includesdeveloping a strong business plan with financial and marketing goalsA coach needs to draw in clients and your marketing efforts may take the formof word of mouth referrals, presenting your services to outreach and aftercare coordinators at treatment centers, offering free coaching sessions, networking with Employee Assistance Associations, publishingblogs, writing articles, giving free talks, and having a website (Killeen, 2013).

Starting your own business as a recovery coach is not for everyone. Another option is to seek a position with an agency or organization. As noted above, the opportunities are expanding as organizations are creating more positions. Common internet databases (such as Monster.com and HotJobs.com) are a good starting points for job openings; however, many terms are used for the title of a recovery coach including peer support specialist, peer mentor, recovery support practitioner, care manager or recovery specialist.

Networking is essential and maybe your best source of referrals, especially if you connect with other professionals to create a complete treatment team for your clients. This can be done in a formal manner with social networking sites such as LinkedIn and Facebook, or an informal manner such as attending trainings, conferences, and professional development. Each of these activities will open up your professional network. In addition to other professionals, your clients will be a strong referral source and maintaining relationships with them after their time with you can lead to many other opportunities.

References

Alcoholics Anonymous (2002). *The Big Book* (4th ed.). New York, NY: Alcoholics Anonymous World Services, Inc.

Armstrong, P. (2006). *The practice of counseling.* Melbourne: Thomson Higher Education.

American Society of Addiction Medicine (2013). About ASAM. ASAM: *The Voice of Addiction Medicine.* www.asam.org/about-us/about.asam

Bartlett, E. (1986). Advocacy skills and strategies for patient education managers. *Patient Education and Counseling, 8,* 397-405.

Center for Substance Abuse Treatment (1999). *Brief Interventions and Brief Therapies for Substance Abuse. Treatment Improvement Protocol (TIP) Series, No. 34.* Rockville, MD: Substance Abuse and Mental Health Services Administration.

Buncher, B. (2009). Loving mirror family recovery coaching. *Family Recovery Resources, LLC.* Retrieved July 10, 2013 from www.familyrecoveryresources.com.

Castonguay, L. G., Constantino, M. J., Holtforth, M. G. (2006). The working alliance: Where are we and where should we go? *Psychotherapy: Theory, Research, Practice, Training, Vol 43(3),* 271-279. doi:10.1037/0033-3204.43.3.271

Center for Substance Abuse Treatment (2009). *What are Peer Recovery Support Services? HHS Publication No. (SMA) 09-4454.* Rockville, MD: Substance Abuse and Mental Health Services Administration.

Connors, G. J., Donovan, D. M., & DiClemente, C. C. (2001). Substance abuse treatment and the stages of chage: Selecting and planning interventions. New York, NY: The Guildford Press.

Copeland, M.E. (2012). The Wellness Recovery Action Plan (WRAP). *Copeland Center for Wellness and Recovery.* Retrieved July 17, 2013 from http://copelandcenter.com/what- wrap/history-wrap.

Dual Recovery Anonymous (2009). Dual diagnosis or co-occurring disorders. *Dual Recovery Anonymous.* Retrieved July 29, 2013 from http://www.draonline.org/dual_diagnosis.html.

Egan, G. (2010). *The skilled helper (9th ed.).* Belmont, CA: Cengage Learning.

Freedman, M. N. & McCaughan, A. M. (2008). HIPAA for dummies: A practitioner's guide. In G.R. Walz, J.C. Blueuer, & R. K. Yep (Eds). *Compelling counseling interventions: Celebrating VISTAS' fifth anniversary* (pp. 305-312), Ann Arbor, MI: Counseling Outfitters.

Granfield, R. & Cloud, W. (1999). *Coming clean: Overcoming addiction without treatment.* New York: New York University Press.

Grohol, J. (2009). 15 Common Cognitive Distortions. *Psych Central.* Retrieved July 31, 2013, from http://psychcentral.com/lib/15-common-cognitive-distortions/0002153

Grohol, J. (2009). Fixing Cognitive Distortions. *Psych Central.* Retrieved July 31, 2013, from http://psychcentral.com/lib/fixing-cognitive-distortions/0002154

Guthmann, D. (1999). *Models of alcohol and other drug treatment for consideration when working with deaf and hard of hearing individuals.* Minneapolis: Minnesota Chemical Dependency Program for Deaf and Hard of Hearing Individuals.

Hammond, W. (2010).Principles of strength-based practice.*Resiliency Initiatives*.Retrieved July 29, 2013 from http://www.ayscbc.org/Principles%20of%20Strength-2.pdf.

Hazelden Foundation (2013). Modified Mini-Screen. Retrieved from http://www.bhevolution.org/public/screening_tools.page?menuheader=4

IC&RC (2013).About IC&RC.*IC&RC Leading the world in credentialing.* Retrieved from www.internationalcredentialing.org/about

International Coach Federation. (2013). Core Competencies.*ICF: International Coach Federation.* Retrieved from http://www.coachfederation.org/credential/landing.cfm?ItemNumber=2206&navItemNumber=576

International Coach Federation. (2013). Ethics & Regulation.*ICF: International Coach Federation.* Retrieved fromhttp://www.coachfederation.org/about/ethics.aspx?ItemNumber=850&navItemNumber=621

Killeen, M. (2013).*Recovery coaching: A guide to coaching people in recovery from addictions.* Laurel Springs, NJ: MK/RC Publishing.

Kottler, J. A. (2000). *Introduction to therapeutic counseling: Voices from the field.* (4th ed.). Belmont, CA: Wadsworth.

Kunkel, T. (2012).*Substance abuse and confidentiality: 42 CFR Part 2.* Williamsburg, VA: National Center for State Courts.

Laudet, A. & William, W. (2008).Recovery capital as prospective predictor of sustained recovery, life satisfaction and stress among former poly-substance users.*Substance Use Misuse, 43* (1), 27-54.

Myers and Briggs Foundation (2013).MBTI basics.Myers and Briggs Foundation.Retrieved July 20, 2013 from http://www.myersbriggs.org/my-mbti-personality-type/mbti-basics/.

McLellan, A. T., Hagan, T. A., Levine, M., Gould, F., Meyers, K. &Bencivengo, M., et al. (1998). Research report: Supplemental social services improve outcomes in public addiction treatment. *Addiction, 93*(10), 1489-1499.

Meyer, P. J. (2003). Attitude is everything: If you want to succeed above and beyond. Waco, TX: Meyer Resource Group, Inc.

Mid-Atlantic Addiction Technology Transfer Center, MI Basics, *Motivational Interviewing Website.*Retrieved from www.motivationalinterview.org.

Miller, W. &Rollnick, S. (1991). *Motivational interviewing: Preparing people to change addictive behavior.* New York, NY: Guilford Press.

Mindtools, Ltd. (2013). The Wheel of Life: Finding balance in your life. *Mindtools.*Retrieved from http://www.mindtools.com/pages/article/newHTE_93.htm#

Mitchell, S. (2002). *Can love last? The fate of romance over time.* New York: Norton.

National Alliance on Mental Illness (2013).Substance abuse and co-occurring disorders.*National Alliance on Mental Illness.*Retrieved August 3, 2013 from http://www.nami.org/Content/NavigationMenu/Hearts_and_Minds/Smoking_Cessation/Substance_Abuse_and_Co-occurring_Disorders.htm.

National Association of Drugs and Alcohol Interventionists.(n.d.).NADAI Certification.Retrieved from http://www.nadai.us/ethics.php.

OptumHealth (2011). [poster presentation] Association for Community Mental Health Administration Summit. New Orleans, LA.

Pawelczyk, J. (2012). "No stories, no self": Co-constructing personal narratives in the psychotherapy session. *Poznan Studies in Contemporary Linguistics, 48*, 1-21.

Purdue University (n.d.). Everything you ever wanted to know about case notes. *Student Resources.*Retrieved from http://www.purdue.edu/hhs/hdfs/engagement/documents/MFT_forms/Student/Resources/Casenote.PDF

Torbay& Southern Devon Health & Care (2013).*Recovery Capital Workshops.* Retrieved July 17, 2013 from http://www/tsdhc.nhs.uk/publications/TSDHC/Recovery%20Capital%20Workshops%20Leaflet.pdf

Recovery Coaches International (2013).Core competencies.*Recovery Coaches International: The voice of choice for recovery and beyond.* Retrieved from http://www.recoverycoaching.org/content.aspx?page_id=22&club_id=263697&module_id=142736

Recovery Coaches International (2013). What is recovery coaching.*Recovery Coaches International: The voice of choice for recovery and beyond.* Retrieved July 7, 2013 from http://www.recoverycoaching.org/content.aspx?page_id=22&club_id=263697&module_id=142729

Harrington, S. (2011). National Association of Peer Specialists.*Recovery to Practice Weekly Highlights, (2)* 21. Retrieved from http://www.samhsa.gov/recoverytoPractice/Resources/2011_weekly/2011_06_09/wh_2011_06_09.html

Recovery within Reach (2013).History of the recovery movement.*Recovery Within Reach.*Retrieved July 3, 2013 from http://www.recoverywithinreach.org/Recovery/history.

Rothman, J. & Sager, S. (1998).*Case management: Integrating individual and community practice.* (2nded.). Upper Saddle River, NJ: Pearson.

Spengler, P. M., Strohmer, D. C., Dixon, D. N., &Shivy, V. A. (1995). A scientist-practitioner model of psychological assessment: Implications for training, practice and research. *The Counseling Psychologist 23:* 506-534. doi: 10.1177/0011000095233009

National Alliance on Mental Illness (2013).Becoming a self-advocate.*Strength of Us.*Retrieved July 13, 2013 from http://strengthofus.org/pages/view/156/.

Substance Abuse and Mental Health Services Administration, Division of Pharmacologic Therapies (2013). Medication-Assisted Treatment (MAT).*Medication-Assisted Treatment for Substance Use Disorders.*Retrieved from http://dpt.samhsa.gov/index.aspx

Substance Abuse and Mental Health Services Administration.(2012). *SAMHSA's Working Definition of Recovery* (Recovery Support Initiative PEP12-RECDEF). Washington, DC: U.S. Government Printing Office. Retrieved from http://store.samhsa.gov/product/SAMHSA-s-Working-Definition-of-Recovery/PEP12-RECDEF

Substance Abuse and Mental Health Services Administration.(2012, September 4).September: Building Communities of Recovery: How Community-Based Partnerships and Recovery Support Organizations Make Recovery Work. *National Recovery Month.* Webcast retrieved from http://www.recoverymonth.gov/Resources-Catalog/2012/Webcast/09-How-CommunityBased-Partnerships-and-Recovery-Support-Organizations-Make-Recovery-Work.aspx

Substance Abuse and Mental Health Services Administration, Office of Applied Studies, National Survey on Drug Use and Health (2009).

Substance Abuse and Mental Health Services Administration, Policy Research Associates (1998). Program Summary: Women, Co Occurring Disorders and Violence Study. Retrieved from http://www.wcdvs.com/publications/default.asp

Center for Substance Abuse Treatment (1999). *Treatment of adolescents with substance use disorders.* Treatment Improvement Protocol (TIP) Series, No 32. Rockville, MD: Substance Abuse and Mental Health Services Administration.

White, W., the PRO-ACT Ethics Workgroup, with legal discussion by Popovits R. & Donohue, B. (2007). *Ethical Guidelines for the Delivery of Peer-based Recovery Support Services.* Philadelphia: Philadelphia Department of Behavioral Health and Mental Retardation Services.

White, W. (1998). *Slaying the dragon: The history of addiction treatment and recovery in America.* Bloomington, IL: Chestnut Health Systems.

White, W. & Cloud, W. (2008). Recovery capital: A primer for addictions professionals. *Counselor, 9*(5), 22-27.

White, W. L. (2008). Recovery management and recovery-oriented systems of care: Scientific rationale and promising practices. Northeast Addiction Technology Transfer Center, the Great Lakes Addiction Technology Transfer Center, and the Philadelphia Department of Behavioral Health and Mental Retardation Services. Philadelphia: Philadelphia Department of Behavioral Health and Mental Retardation Services.

Contributors

Dr. Laura Pipoly

Laura Pipoly earned her Bachelor of Arts in Psychology from Hiram College. She then graduated summa cum laude with her master's degree from Youngstown State University in education in both school counseling and clinical mental health counseling. She is a Professional Counselor (PC) and a certified K-12 school counselor. In addition, Laura is recognized as a National Board Certified Counselor. Laura completed her doctorate degree from Nova Southeastern University with a dual concentration in instructional technology and distance education (ITDE) and special education. Her dissertation focuses on distance education counseling students and is titled Counseling Students Perceptions towards the Efficacy of Online Counseling.

Laura enjoys teaching courses for Grand Canyon University and University of Phoenix. Most recently, Laura authored the book foreward to an E-book titled, "Meeting the Challenges of Bipolar Disorder: Self Help Strategies that Work!"

Trudi Griffin, MS, LPC-I

Trudi Griffin, is a former psychiatric technician and now a Licensed Professional Counselor Intern currently works for her supervisor's private practice in Red Oak, TX, where she provides counseling for people recovering from substance abuse, trauma, and other mental health issues.

Ms. Griffin is a graduate of Marquette University (Milwaukee, WI), and holds a Master's of Science in Clinical Mental Health Counseling: Addictions and Mental Health. As a clinic manager and counselor at The Bridge Health Clinics & Research Centers in Milwaukee, WI, she provided trauma-informed counseling to individuals utilizing evidence-based therapies including CBT, DBT, REBT, and Seeking Safety, and facilitated substance abuse groups utilizing SMART Recovery, CBT, REBT, Seeking Safety, Motivational Interviewing, and 12 Step interventions. She also counseled survivors of sexual assault and conducted groups for survivors in recovery.

In Eddy County, NM, Trudi served as an Adolescent Intensive Outpatient Therapist and provided counseling to adolescent drug court participants and their families, using Moral Reconation Therapy (MRT). While there, she also coordinated a new adolescent intensive outpatient substance abuse program based upon The Matrix for Teens and Young Adults, which included groups, individual and family therapy.

www.ingramcontent.com/pod-product-compliance
Lightning Source LLC
Chambersburg PA
CBHW081724270326
41933CB00017B/3295